KEIJUTSUKAI
AIKIDO
Japanese Art of Self-Defense

by
Thomas H. Makiyama

Editor: Gregory Lee
Graphic Design: Dung Pham

Art Production: Mary Schepis

© 1983 Ohara Publications, Inc.
All rights reserved
Printed in the United States of America
Library of Congress Catalog Card Number 83-61559
ISBN: 0-89750-092-X

Sixth Printing 1988

WARNING

OHARA ▯ PUBLICATIONS, INCORPORATED
BURBANK, CALIFORNIA

DEDICATION

To my loyal Japanese and foreign students, including the active supporters of our Keijutsukai, in Tokyo and abroad.

ACKNOWLEDGEMENTS

I am deeply grateful to my many students for their wholehearted support, not only in the compiling of this book, but also for their continuing, intense dedication and loyalty in support of the objectives of the Keijutsukai system. To those students, particularly, who were involved with the difficult photographic illustrations; your willingness to give so many hours and days of your time is sincerely appreciated—to name all would be next to impossible. Special thanks to Hisato Kawasaki, Tomio Murakami, Yasuyuki Sakai, Kenneth Long, Larry Novak, Noriko Takahashi, Lloyd Kumagai, Richard Savage, George Neal, Yoshinori Nakamura, Michiko Ishizu. To Ray Naegele, whose ready wit contributed greatly to the morale of the photographic sessions. Also, Leslie Yamada, always content to remain silent but ready to assist positively at all times. Last, but not least, to my wonderful wife, Yoko, who has constantly preferred to remain in the background, yet was always a source of inspiration and encouragement during the preparation of this book.

ABOUT THE AUTHOR

Thomas Makiyama is a man of many hats: martial artist, businessman, journalist, teacher and ex-law enforcement investigator. He has been intensely involved in the martial arts for 35 years, both as a black belt instructor and as a freelance writer for such publications as *Black Belt* magazine.

He is believed to be the only native American to have officially attained an eighth-dan (degree) ranking in aikido along with a certification of *shihan* (master teacher) through one of the two recognized Japanese aikido organizations in Japan.

Born in Hawaii in 1928, Makiyama served in the U.S. Eighth Army, stationed after World War II in Japan and later in Korea. He also worked for several years in the Army's Criminal Investigation Division (CID) in Tokyo, Yokohama, and Korea—the latter, during the Outbreak.

For 20 years Makiyama owned and operated his own travel agency in Honolulu. While he lived in Hawaii, Makiyama was instrumental in forming the first official branch of the Aikido Yoshinkan outside of Japan during the 1950s. He also authored the first book in English on aikido during the same decade.

Makiyama now resides in Tokyo, making extensive use of his bilingual abilities as an independent consultant to Japanese and American businesses. He continues to help promote all the martial arts there and in the U.S.

The Keijutsukai Aikido was founded by Makiyama early in 1979 in Tokyo. The first American branch is located in Los Angeles, California.

INTRODUCTION

This book is the culmination of my total observations and experience over the past 35 years concerning the subject of aikido, especially as it pertains to foreign expansion and particularly within the United States.

Following a somewhat meteoric splash abroad during the mid-50s, a series of unfortunate occurrences ensued which progressively eroded the expected growth and popularity of aikido. In an endeavor to set the record straight, I have made an effort to detail some of the major shortcomings, past and present. In essence, the blame should not be placed upon aikido, for it is and has been a highly respected art in the budo cognate. The fault lies with a few individuals within the various schools of aikido—individuals who saw fit to manipulate students and branches for personal gain. This type of thinking can, in part, be attributed to the language and cultural gap often experienced between Japanese and foreigners. From the outset, a thorough public relations effort has been sadly lacking.

Along with existing problems, there were those who attempted to convey aikido techniques through an alleged Zen-like philosophy, accompanied by stunts that incorporated elementary physics and common sense. These advocates insisted that a mysterious source of spiritual strength must be mastered (according to *their* teachings, of course) in order for one to learn the intricate principles of aikido. This is erroneous. These confusing aspects, among several others, affected students and instructors alike in the learning of aikido techniques, producing improper interpretations of aikido principles.

The unfortunate result has been that aikido instruction has perpetuated the status quo, compounded by a growing disillusionment on the part of many long-time supporters of the aikido movement in the U.S., causing a good number of them to leave aikido for good.

The loyalty and dedication of the average American student toward his Japanese headquarters (and their official representatives) is often much more intense than that of the native Japanese students themselves. In some cases, certain lost moral characteristics indicative of the old Japanese budo have been studied in-depth by the American student or instructor. Thus, it is difficult for them to comprehend the so-called differences encountered in the ways of the "modernized" Japanese teacher in relation to what they have been told or read in the past, for the techniques and motivations appear to be diverse in many ways. It can be said that Japanese instructors are today, first and foremost, *Japanese businessmen.*

The Keijutsukai was formed by the author in the hope of making a positive contribution to foreign aikido, and to assist in the reviving of interest in aikido. Since major changes and differences were made, it seemed best to establish a completely new organization and to accept full responsibility for its actions, avoiding accusations of passing the buck, so to speak. The training concepts will be new, and formal training seminars will be scheduled in the near future, both in Japan and the U.S. Having personally experienced the actual trials and tribulations of studying under several native instructors in Japan in past years, I feel confident that I will be in a position to understand the difficult problems ahead involving both sides.

Proponents of other aikido schools may consider some of my statements in this book as being too strong. The problems I have noted, however, exist and should be corrected as soon as possible, for the Keijutsukai firmly believes in working together for the future growth of aikido. To quote from an old American adage, "United we stand, divided we fall." A strong and amicable relationship must be encouraged between all aikido groups and that of other recognized budo schools.

—Thomas H. Makiyama
Tokyo, Japan
November 6, 1982

PUBLISHER'S NOTE

The terminology used to describe basic techniques will often differ from one aikido school to the next. In compiling this text, the author has chosen to avoid confusion by using some of the general terminology employed by the Yoshinkan system—terminology with which most aikidoists will be familiar.

Keep in mind that while many of the techniques in this book *may visually* resemble techniques from other schools, the explanations and execution of each is *radically different* under the Keijutsukai approach. Unless the instructions and photographs are followed carefully, the student will only duplicate the moves through physical force—an undesirable quality in mastering basic Keijutsukai Aikido. *A technique has failed if it requires force for its successful completion.*

For better understanding, English terms have been used wherever possible instead of the native Japanese terms, with the exception of some which are extremely difficult to translate in a shortened version without losing the meaning intended. Further, foreign students of Keijutsukai should make an effort to learn the more commonly used Japanese terms in aikido. A glossary has been included in this text for reference.

AIKIDO: ITS ORIGIN AND
PROGRESS TO DATE

Before delving into the historical origin of aikido, an interpretation of the name is called for. Aikido, as implied by the nature of its unusual movements and techniques, can best be translated roughly as "a way of fitting in," to mentally and physically fit in with the force or movements of another. A state of compatibility forms the essence of aikido techniques and interpretation.

Aikido techniques involve over 2,000 inter-related throws, locks, nerve point attacks, and strikes in a number of ways. This figure can easily be increased when combinations and cross-combinations are taken into account. Due to the sheer number of techniques, it is virtually impossible to name them all. Only a few of the basic techniques, therefore, possess readily identifiable names. Depending upon the school, even these basic names have been slightly altered, mainly between the "soft" and "hard" schools; a further explanation is found elsewhere in the book.

The origin of aikido varies, depending upon whom you ask. However, the generally accepted version credits an unknown samurai retainer, a master of the sword and jujitsu, who belonged to the Shinra-Saburo-Yoshimitsu-Minamoto clan during the Kamakura Period some 800 years past. He was the originator of *Daito-ryu Aiki jutsu,* the art from which aikido is descended. Contrary to popular belief, the Daito-ryu (school or system) did not limit itself to unarmed self-defense, as the complete system included tactics with the sword and the spear *(yari),* dagger throwing, and other related defenses.

By strict tradition, the art was taught only to a select group of the upper nobility and kept completely secret and separate from the accepted martial arts training undertaken by the *samurai* or warrior class. This was not considered an unusual practice, considering that indiscriminate assassinations were somewhat commonplace during that particularly turbulent period of Japanese history. It was, therefore, imperative that certain key individuals of the nobility be protected from physical harm whether or not official protection was provided. Daito-ryu, after being retained by the Minamoto clan for some 200 years, was subsequently passed to the clan of Shingen Takeda, another prominent historical figure, who ruled the area of Koshu (known today as Yamanashi Prefecture). To date, the art has been in the possession of the Takeda descendants. Although little-known, it still continues to be taught on a very limited scale in Hokkaido.

Morihei Uyeshiba, the late aikido master and an accomplished swordsman in his own right, undertook studies in the Daito-ryu techniques through the personal tutelage of Sokaku Takeda—the legitimate successor to the art at the time. Uyeshiba proved to be an apt pupil, quickly mastering the techniques of this intricate art. Following completion of his studies, Uyeshiba left to teach on his own, renaming the newly founded system, *aikido*. He is further credited with the introduction and, in some cases, improvements found in the modern version of aikido—many of which greatly improved upon the old Daito-ryu techniques. The name or term aikido, therefore, is actually less than 100 years old.

In keeping with traditional practices, Uyeshiba did not attempt to conduct large classes for the general public, preferring instead to teach only a few select students. According to several sources, some of the officers of the *Kempeitai* (Japanese Military Police) and the Navy were reported to be among a special group of military men chosen to undertake aikido training under the personal supervision of Uyeshiba. In the years immediately after WWII, aikido, along with many of the other martial arts, was banned automatically under the Occupation, as these arts were deemed too militaristic and closely entrenched with the former wartime military regime. In time, however, these directives were rescinded, made possible mainly through the efforts of the police authorities (which included many active judo and kendo practitioners), and the arts made a gradual revival. Uyeshiba was finally persuaded to open up aikido training to the public around that time. Prominent among his early proteges was Gozo Shioda, director and chief instructor of the Aikido Yoshinkan and a top-ranked ninth dan (the highest officially-recognized ranking conferred by the late Uyeshiba). Shioda's Yoshinkan system has been the authorized aikido training for officers of the Tokyo Metropolitan Police Department for the past 20 years; one of Shioda's proteges, an eighth dan, is presently chief aikido instructor for the Department.

Today, aikido systems fall into two general categories: the "soft" and "hard" schools—a phrase coined by the author during the late 1950s to describe the existing aikido training. The "soft" school is typified by the Uyeshiba system, headed by the late master's son, Kishomaru Uyeshiba. The advocate of the "hard" school is best typified by the Aikido Yoshinkan system under Shioda. Several lesser-known, small aikido schools have been formed over the years, with the majority being offshoots from the Uyeshiba school. The major differences in the two schools mentioned are in the area of training methods and approach; however, both are essentially similar insofar as aikido principles are concerned during the basic phases. The "soft" approach emphasizes rather exaggerated movements, concentrating very heavily upon theoretical attack situations; defensive movements are attuned to the attacker, who executes a prearranged strike so that the defender can successfully move in a set pattern. Since the attacker assumes that the defender must be permitted to move in a theoretical pattern arranged beforehand, the forcefulness of the strike or attack leaves much to be desired. The same type of training is repeated in a listless, monotonous pattern. Its effectiveness under actual situations is doubtful on the part of the average student. The school is also a proponent of the so-called *ki* principle, where concentration is allegedly centered at a point just above the navel, resulting in a "spiritual" source of undefined strength necessary in the execution of aikido movements and techniques. Considerable stress is placed on the ki concept.

The "hard" system, on the other hand, relies quite heavily on being able to duplicate a set pattern for a given movement or technique, as demonstrated by an instructor. Quite often, force is substituted for the natural flow of movement and execution; it is more like the jujitsu of old, where a static form of attack and defense was taught. The attack situations, however, are much more realistic than that of the "soft" school; a typical "defender" at one time, sustained a fracture of the forearm by blocking an attacker's overhand strike—confirming that force was used against force and not by flowing with the flow of the attacker's force. The hard school has also utilized the *atemi* (strike) as a diversionary tactic, along with the follow-up of an appropriate aikido technique—the first school in aikido to have done so. (The soft school in recent years has also incorporated the atemi concept by utilizing special hand protectors.) Although practical to some degree, the hard school still maintains the standard practice of following set patterns and theoretical defenses, utilizing strength to accomplish its end results. However, they do not advocate the ki concept along the lines of the soft schools.

Aikido Development Throughout the Western World

Aikido was initially introduced in the U.S. during the early 1950s, commencing in Hawaii and California. The public was duly impressed by the often spectacular locks and throws executed by expert instructors from Japan during demonstrations—techniques which apparently involved very little effort. From the outset, aikido schools did very well, having caught the public's fancy and interest; for a time even some of the other arts began to introduce the art along with their own! A favorable growth trend continued for a few years. European countries have followed a similar growth pattern, but on a lesser scale.

With the approach of the 30-year mark since aikido's debut on the international scene, the results thus far have been less than gratifying. Instead of the expected firm growth and establishment of the aikido movement, the opposite situation exists. Schools are still in operation, but little or no organized publicity surrounds their activity. Interest in aikido has been on the decline in recent years and a sad state of stagnation has resulted. Some of the causes are inherent: internal strife, complacency, personal pride, technical considerations—all problems which have cropped up over the years within all aikido groups. In sharp contrast, other arts have succeeded in overtaking aikido in popularity during this period.

The aikido movement in Japan, however, has enjoyed favorable growth over the years, and popularity has not yet peaked. The various media often take up the subject, along with regular coverage of the other arts; a good indicator of equal interest. In time, aikido abroad will once again occupy its rightful niche, with the assistance and support of the many dedicated and sincere students and instructors who wish to continue their studies into the fascinating subject of aikido.

CONTENTS

KEIJUTSUKAI AIKIDO

The Keijutsukai (Police/Security Techniques Association) was officially established in February, 1980, in Tokyo, Japan, although the actual training of students commenced during the early part of 1979. The term *keijutsukai* is an acronym derived from Japanese *kanji* characters in the basic sense. However, many other factors were taken into serious consideration in arriving at this specific designation for the permanent identification of the school.

Keijutsukai Aikido and its counterpart, Keijutsu (a highly specialized method of self-defense for law enforcement personnel), is an innovative concept of teaching and learning aikido. The Keijutsukai emphasizes a rational and practical approach to the subject, differing in many ways from that of conventional teachings to date. A detailed, no-nonsense explanation of the techniques is the main feature. The students are considered and treated as individuals. Techniques are not taught by rote, a common deficiency of aikido schools over the years. The Keijutsukai takes a realistic view of physical limitations, age, and psychological factors which play an important part in a student's ability to practice and learn aikido successfully. They are not forced to keep up with others, but are encouraged to develop at their own pace—in all cases, under the personal supervision of the instructor or his assistants. Beyond the basic foundation-building exercises and movements, techniques are taught at a rapid pace, but well within the capabilities of a given student. Students and teachers of the conventional schools of aikido will readily note the areas of difference by reading through this book, including the explanations of the techniques.

The Keijutsukai was created to restore some long-overdue requirements which have been sadly lacking in the teaching and learning of aikido, particularly in foreign countries. To cite a few examples: aside from a few individuals, the aikido schools have very seldom participated together in exhibitions, preferring instead to conduct their own demonstrations, thus, severely limiting an impartial view of aikido by the uninitiated. Aikido exhibitions have often included alleged techniques that are mainly stunts and trick throws; in reality, nothing more than elementary physics. At the other end of the extreme, students are erroneously led to believe that a mystical source of spiritual power lies at the root of aikido, and that this particular concept must be mastered through a prescribed form of concentration which borders on Zen Buddhism. At times, deliberate force is utilized in attempting to execute a prescribed technique, completely disregarding the basic aikido principles of *ma-ai* and *marui*.

These types of problems are due to insufficient knowledge or explanations by foreign instructors possessing a limited background on aikido. A long tenure in aikido membership does not necessarily qualify one as an "instructor," even though he may have attended a so-called refresher course for a month or two in Japan. Brief corrective training cannot possibly undo bad habits picked up over the years; one will revert to doing the same things once *proper* supervision is no longer available. Others have been complacent, preferring to live on past reputation; a *dan* (black belt degree) is usually granted by virtue of seniority rather than actual proficiency and thorough knowledge of aikido, including teaching ability.

Over the years, it has been established that many foreign students of aikido are, in many ways, far more dedicated in their studies of the art (attempting to duplicate the traditions and its courtesies) than the average Japanese student of today. Unfortunately, this all-out dedication and loyalty toward their Japanese headquarters has not been fully appreciated nor reciprocated, in fact, at times, completely misunderstood. Commercialism has taken precedence over everything else, including improvement, progress, and quality control of the art; to attain their financial objectives, foreign branches and individuals are often exploited to the fullest. High moral standards of character and integrity, so often *preached* by the top-ranked Japanese instructors of aikido, become mere *words*.

Sadly disillusioned students and instructors in the past had little choice: either endure the situation or leave the organization. Departure automatically indicated a termination of aikido activities and promotions as recognized by a Japan school. Thus, the majority have elected to remain for the sake of learning aikido to some degree, and have quietly learned to grin and bear it. This is a deplorable state of conditions permitting the further deterioration of aikido growth. Half-hearted interest on the part of students will not help develop excellent instructors.

While it is true that many of these problems resulted from an initial cultural gap (compounded by meek acceptance without question), foreign students and instructors should have asked, "Why?" The Western mind is an inquisitive one by nature, but in the case of aikido direct questions appear to have been avoided over the years, perhaps due to the language barrier and subtle forms of brainwashing. Foreign students undergoing refresher training for a month or two in Japan have experienced the feeling of being lost in a morass. After a couple of days, one is left to fend for himself and to mingle with the regular Japanese classes. Without the availability of a bilingual person, the visitor becomes highly frustrated. Asking "why" brings forth an unclear explanation. (Japanese students, as a rule, *do not ask* pointed questions, and are content *to do* as they are told.)

Lest the reader be misled, the Keijutsukai is not meant to be a perfect system. It is hoped that the Keijutsukai can make a small contribution through its own efforts to offset some of these existing problems and renew the interest of active and inactive students.

Since its inception, the Keijutsukai has striven to convey a sense of mutual understanding and trust among students of mixed cultural backgrounds; classes consist of native Japanese, Americans, and Europeans. The experiment has proven to be a success, with a highly motivated and dedicated group of students forming over the past four years. Aside from a thorough and practical grounding in Keijutsukai Aikido, students are also taught the craft of teaching—including budo courtesies. They have been instilled with a feeling of *esprit de corps* and a sense of friendship between *sempai* and *kohai* (upper and lower classmen). Students are encouraged to develop tolerance of other recognized, non-aikido schools, and to work actively within their communities to jointly project a favorable image of the arts to the general public, often by sponsoring mixed demonstrations of different schools of aikido and other systems, such as judo and karate.

Aikido, as taught by the Keijutsukai system, considers it a necessity to understand the existence of other non-aikido arts in relation to its own techniques; thus, practice includes avoidance of possible attack situations. It believes that the old repetitive and theoretical concepts of so-called aikido self-defense methods are outmoded for the average student. A Japanese instructor, for example, works with theoretical attack and defense patterns, unaware that the actual street situation is quite different. They have not encountered first hand, say, a knife wielder or a handgun.

Since over 95 percent of the normal training in conventional aikido is based upon ancient sword-handling methods and related theories, the modern form of aikido as it is leaves much to be desired. Combinations and cross-combinations of aikido techniques, including counters of said movements are rarely if ever taught to students over a period of time, since many of the instructors themselves are *not familiar* with them. Students of the Keijutsukai system are gradually taught various forms of defenses, as deemed necessary.

Keijutsukai Aikido attempts to strip the subject of aikido of its deliberately mysterious aura perpetrated over the past 30 years in Western countries. Aikido is effective, with its related locks and throws, and is often painful and dangerous to the receiver(s); however, in spite of the apparent difficulties in the learning of aikido, the subject may be successfully pursued by anyone observing three simple rules. They are:

1. Practice.
2. *More* practice.
3. *Still* more practice.

Along with these, the following factors are also important from the standpoint of mental outlook:

—Learning to maintain a relaxed mental and physical attitude.

—Developing a sense of humor.

—Training oneself in mental discipline for the building of self-confidence.

Relaxation is generally assumed to indicate physical rest, but the Keijutsukai emphasizes a state of mental relaxation, for the mind controls the feeling of either being tired or active from a physical standpoint. A good sense of humor is desirable in learning Keijutsukai Aikido, as many of its movements and techniques can be a rather frustrating experience for the first-timer. A student must learn to pace himself, and not become easily angered if a certain movement cannot be mastered in one or two sessions. Errors should be taken in stride, and once the student learns to laugh at minor frustrations, he will make positive progress. By fully understanding these relaxation and humor aspects in Keijutsukai training one will begin to master the last; that is, self or mental discipline.

The advance study of Keijutsukai Aikido is quite different from that of conventional systems. Attacks and defensive situations are geared more toward realistic occurrences, and simulated during actual practice sessions in the dojo. An attacker, for example, will be severely chastised for taking a fall if, obviously, the technique was *not effective*—a common fault in aikido training. Exhibitions and demonstrations explain Keijutsukai beforehand to prepare an audience, detailing the reasons why competitions, as found in karate or judo, cannot be held. Circus or trick-like throws, in general, are not advocated by the Keijutsukai, and are limited by degree, to demonstrate how aikido may be utilized under realistic conditions or multiple attacks.

This book was prompted by numerous individuals who have expressed a desire for a volume which would shed additional light on the subject of aikido by doing away with mysterious philosophy.

It is the intention of the Keijutsukai to eventually form branches and affiliates in other countries. A completely new method of teaching, based on a personalized method of visual media is being contemplated—a first to utilize this new means, and future training seminars are scheduled. Additional information concerning the School may be obtained by contacting:

KEIJUTSUKAI (Japan Headquarters)
Shimbashi Shinwa Bldg. 4F
5-15, 4-chome, Shimbashi, Minato-Ku,
Tokyo 105, JAPAN

Keijutsukai Aikido (U.S. Branch)
1217 Torrance Blvd.
Torrance, California 90502
(213) 323-4164

FUNDAMENTAL PRINCIPLES OF AIKIDO

Proper execution and understanding of basic aikido movements can be difficult for beginning students unless one has a grasp of certain fundamental principles. The diagrams in this section (pages 22-23) are intended to help the student visualize some important ideas about balance and movement.

The first illustration in this section is similar to that of an ordinary compass. For the moment, we will study the eight directional points indicated. These points may be utilized to disturb the normal balance of an opponent, provided that a technique is executed in the correct manner. Try this experiment: Have someone stand with both feet firmly planted, say, east and west, while facing north or south. Now, place your fingertip(s) or the palm of either hand against his back between the shoulder blades. A slight push or pull from north to south (or vice versa) will easily unbalance your assistant. But, his balance will be naturally strong along the east-west axis. In this event, however, his balance may still be broken by merely changing the direction of the push or pull toward any of the *remaining six points* illustrated. Example: Place your palm or fingertip(s) against one of the shoulders of your assistant and push steadily toward the opposite side (east-to-west/west-to-east); notice that a decidedly strong resistance is encountered? Now, suddenly change the pushing action in the direction of any of the remaining six points and your assistant will immediately sustain a loss of normal balance. Pulling achieves the same result. A quick, smooth combination of push and pull can also accomplish the same results. Instructors and students of judo are familiar with this, since they too are required to understand the "directional" principles.

The illustrations which have been included in this section indicate some of the basic directions in which an opponent may be unbalanced and subsequently thrown. A careful perusal of the diagrams will readily disclose these directional principles. The unbroken lines are the primary route, and the broken lines, some of the possible secondary directions utilized to unbalance or throw an opponent. Note that curves and circular paths are heavily emphasized in the majority of the illustrations, rather than a straight path from the beginning to the end of a given movement. These movements may also follow an upward or downward path, in *conjunction* with the primary or secondary routes. Throws, however, may be executed along a straight path, once one is fully proficient in the movements and is able to understand the *marui* (circular) and *ma-ai* (distance) principles of aikido.

Directional movements should be executed in a smooth manner, without pauses or jerks. In certain instances, an opponent will resist efforts to offset his balance, thus, the initiator must move smoothly and in one continuous motion—in any direction—to keep his opponent constantly off balance until a proper throwing position arises. By moving continuously in the primary and secondary directions, and changing suddenly when resistance is encountered, the opponent will ultimately lose his balance. Example: Move an opponent in a line directed along one of the diagrams. As a slight resistance is encountered, execute a smooth but sudden change of direction indicated by one of the secondary (broken) lines in the same illustration. If the change of direction is done correctly, your opponent will be unable to react fast enough to recover his balance. It then becomes a relatively simple process to employ a throw or an applicable technique, with a minimum of effort to obtain the maximum effect desired. These diagrams and the following paragraphs of this section must be thoroughly understood and practiced diligently until the initiator (the student) can execute these movements in a natural manner, from purely reflex action. This will entail time and patience, and can best be learned under the personal supervision of a competent aikido instructor, preferably Keijutsukai trained. Merely reading about aikido will not suffice, and this book is no exception to the rule. It is recommended that this book be used to supplement personal instruction if at all possible.

Marui or the circular principle of aikido and *ma-ai* or the distance principle are two inseparable aspects of aikido—they are considered the essence of true aikido movements.

THE DIRECTIONAL PRINCIPLE OF AIKIDO

The illustrations below (showing the eight cardinal directions of the compass) and on the opposite page illustrate some of the basic directions in which an opponent can be unbalanced and then thrown with a sudden change of direction. The unbroken lines represent primary routes, the broken lines secondary routes.

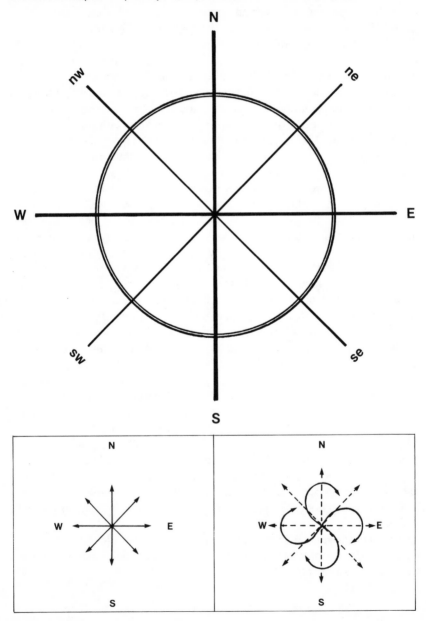

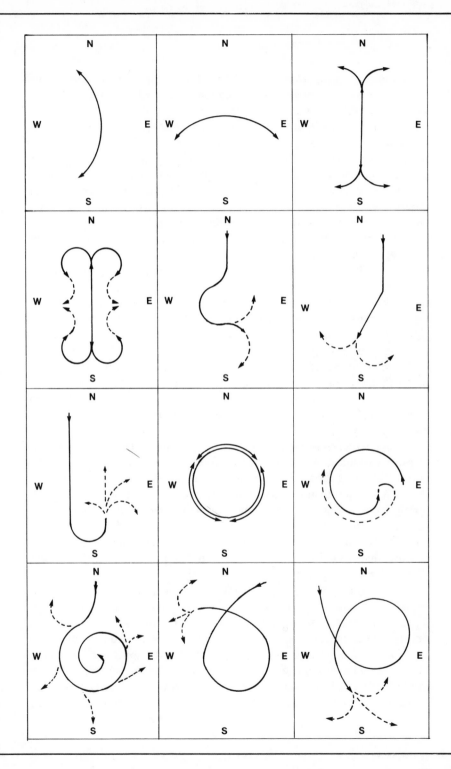

A forceful attack from the front travels a set line. Should the receiver meet the force head-on, a collision situation is inevitable. However, if, at the very instant the oncoming force is expected to make actual contact, the receiver steps aside slightly, the opponent's balance is disturbed in the line of his own force. In moving aside, the receiver pivots away from the line of force while using his own hands to guide the opponent's body into the direction (circular) of the pivot. At this point, the opponent has no choice but to follow the movement of the receiver due to his loss of balance. This pivoting movement of the body and hands is called marui. The majority of aikido techniques and movements employ the circular maneuver to a large degree. To the uninitiated, the movements appear ballet-like with their light, circular series of motions.

Another important factor must be considered—the ma-ai rule. Without observing the proper ma-ai between the opponent and the initiator at all times, movements and techniques become ineffective. Gauging the appropriate ma-ai in a given situation takes a while, for several things must be considered: the size and strength of an opponent, along with the initiator's sense of speed, timing, and coordination. Organized practice will help. Ma-ai also refers to the effective operating distance between the initiator and the opponent *after* initial body contact is made. The moves of the initiator must be *fluid* and the technique completed smoothly in *one continuous movement.* Without flexibility of the mind and body, ma-ai and marui will not mesh properly.

To maintain stable body position, the *koshi* (hips) are very important to consider. To illustrate: An opposing force is drawn around and into a vortex; in aikido, the initiator represents the central point. The action is like that of a whirlpool, and is called centripetal force. At the other end, the opposing force spirals out, struggling away from the central vortex—this is centrifugal force. Since the force must be redirected in a single well-coordinated move (without the initiator destroying his own balance), it is imperative that a *controlled* center of gravity be maintained *during* a continuous circular movement.

Try this experiment: From a stationary position, take a step either forward or backward. In both instances, the weight shifts naturally toward the direction of the step, as encountered routinely in walking. Repeat the action, only this time, imagine that you are stepping out or back from the middle of your *lower back* instead of your foot. Notice that the upper and lower parts of your body move in *unison,* without the natural shifting of body weight as in the first case. In the latter, the center of gravity is controlled, and the move was executed not with the foot itself but with the *whole body moving as one.* A student of Keijutsukai Aikido must practice diligently to lower the koshi until the control of his center of gravity becomes second nature. Strong koshi placement is a must in order for one to become adept in the techniques of Keijutsukai Aikido—strive to perfect this area.

Kokyu-ho (Way of Compatibility)

This particular term has caused a great deal of confusion and misunderstanding among aikido practitioners over the years. One reason is that *kokyu* was translated literally to mean "breathing." Although correct in the pure sense, the kanji characters also denote another interpretation meaning a state of compatibility. The latter meaning would be the appropriate one in the context of aikido principles under the Keijutsukai system. Japanese terms utilized in aikido (and within some of the other major arts) are ones with which even the average Japanese may not be acquainted with—names devised specially for a given system of martial art. To add to the confusion, certain aikido schools and instructors have chosen to explain the existence of kokyu with a mysterious Zen-like philosophy.

Kokyu-ho is a method of practice whereby one undergoes physical and mental exercises through repetitive movements and techniques. *Eventually,* the student begins to feel the movements of an opponent. An example: Let's assume that an opponent is firmly grasping the initiator's wrist. Instinctively, the normal tendency is to fight back, either by resisting or attempting to pull the captive wrist free. This is force against force, usually culminating in success for the stronger individual. However, through regular practice, it becomes possible for the aikidoist to learn the method of relaxing in mind and body so that he can feel the force being directed upon his wrist and gradually learn to *flow* along the path of the force; in other words, to go with the grain instead of fighting back with strength alone. The flow principle also applies to other types of force, such as strikes or punches. In striking attacks, the matter of actually feeling the force, of course, cannot be readily discerned. Practice will train the aikidoist to react automatically, *providing* that he has mastered to some degree the concepts of marui, ma-ai, and has proper control of his koshi.

The beginning student may encounter considerable difficulties learning the various movements and rules set forth here. This is not unusual. Your ultimate objective is to be able to perform all movements in a continuous and well-timed action without tensing or *forcing* any technique. One should strive to learn with the *body* rather than attempting to *memorize.*

IMPORTANT NOTES ON TRAINING

Practice

It is desirable to schedule a minimum of two sessions weekly—with a two-hour duration per practice period, not including the customary short breaks in-between for resting. There should be ample space to permit the participants to move about and take falls without fear of accidental injuries caused by falling against one another; if space is limited, care must be taken so that the number of participants performing at any given time can move about freely. Others should be awaiting their turn while maintaining a *seiza* (kneeling) position along one side of the mats. Due to the necessity of taking falls, the floor should be lined with judo-type matting.

The practice of aikido is best performed by two individuals working out together. This will insure smooth, continuous progress in lessons. In attempting to practice the techniques described in this book, students are cautioned to observe certain important rules for the prevention of accidental injuries. Some of the more important ones are:

1. The techniques described in this book must be strictly adhered to in every detail. Any attempt to improvise can, and will, lead to injuries.
2. All practice must be conducted with care and a proper sense of responsibility. Keijutsukai Aikido techniques, in particular, can cause considerable pain to the recipient—joints may be dislocated and bones broken with very little exertion. Bear this in mind at all times.

3. Never, in jest, apply the locks and throws described in this book upon someone who is not familiar with aikido, and who cannot properly react to them, including beginning students. The *sempai* or instructor is available to *teach,* not to *impress* others with his ability.
4. A serious student of Keijutsukai Aikido will utilize the knowledge gained only for exercise and actual self-defense situations. (Keijutsukai Aikido encompasses a series of limbering-up and conditioning exercises which are considerably different from other schools of aikido.)
5. Basic types of break and roll-out falls should be mastered before progressing on with techniques, otherwise injuries may result. Some of the falls are discussed in this book. Since falls are basically of the judo type, any good judo instructor can easily train someone in this requirement. There are also a number of excellent English-language books on judo describing falls in detail.

Techniques

Keijutsukai Aikido techniques may *appear* the same as found within other aikido schools. However, the similarity is only visual in that Keijutsukai *is* aikido. The major differences will be found in the manner of explanations, with specific emphasis placed on areas previously ignored: the rationale of aikido, practical approaches, objectives, etc. (Refer to the sections on Fundamental Principles of Aikido and Keijutsukai Aikido.)

Brief examples of these differences are as follows: A hard, frontal strike is not "caught" or "slammed away," for this type of action defeats the intent of aikido in the pure sense. It should be lightly deflected along the initial path or redirected into a natural orbit, in line with the defender's own body movement. The strike may also be redirected and positioned to a point where an appropriate technique may be employed. The movements and techniques must *not* be memorized, but should be learned with the mind and body through natural coordination and body movements that flow or fit in with that of an opponent. Since the attacker is not limited to what he can utilize, the defender must be completely relaxed to be able to react to any type of unexpected move. Attack movements are not "telegraphed" to prepare the defender.

Another difference is in the way certain locking techniques are accomplished. The Keijutsukai method relies heavily on control of the *kokyu* and *koshi* in appplying techniques. Force, per se, is discouraged in completing a technique or movement. Exact imitation of the instructor is not encouraged, and individuals are taught to incorporate the principles implied within the limit of their own capability (including height, weight, age, physical handicap, etc.). As the student progresses with his studies, he is gradually assigned to practice with one of the senior students to sharpen his abilities. Women, too, are not limited to working out among themselves, and are often teamed up with men of equal or higher ability if the student is doing well.

Uniforms

The judo type of practice uniform (*dogi*) is the prescribed wear for aikido practice. Uniform size should be selected with care; it must not be too snug in fit, for laundering will invariably cause some shrinkage of the material. Ideally, the jacket should permit freedom of movement without an unnatural binding under the armpits. The trousers should be about ankle length. Belt size is a matter of personal choice—usually the two ends, after tying, protrude 10-12 inches from the knot. For the beginner, the wearing of the uniform sometimes presents unexpected confusion. The trousers are provided with a draw-string affair, and one or two belt loops (depending on the manufacturer) will be found at the front of the trousers. The two ends of the draw strings are looped through and tied firmly with a bow. Jackets are worn, folded left over right, for both men and women. A simple way of centering the *obi* (belt or sash) is to first determine its center, then placing same against the abdomen. The belt is wrapped around, bringing the two ends back over the hip bone and abdomen. One of the ends must then be inserted from below, looping over both belt overlappings, and an old-fashioned square knot completes the tie—the overlapping prevents the belt from separating during exercises. Belts should be tied in a comfortable manner and not too tightly. Uniforms should be laundered frequently, and try to air out your uniform after each practice.

In aikido, a common sight is the wearing of the *hakama* (much like a skirt), either navy-blue or black, by some of the men and women in a dojo. Depending upon the school, students who have attained a certain level of dan are permitted to wear the hakama, if they so desire. Usually a second or a third dan is the minimum; women, on the other hand, are allowed to wear the hakama after attaining first dan at most schools. The Keijutsukai follows a similar practice. In Japan, unlike the U.S., the hakama is not worn indiscriminately—the Aikido Yoshinkan, for example, very seldom has hakama-clad people on the mats during normal practice; only the chief instructor is so attired. Senior instructors at that school are usually observed in their hakama during official functions. In general, the hakama should be worn only during special events, and not considered as a regular practice uniform, for this lessens the distinction of wearing the traditional hakama.

Dojo Courtesies

As in all martial arts, aikido requires the observance of basic budo courtesies and a certain amount of common sense in the dojo.

Upon entering or leaving the dojo, everyone is expected to pause at the entrance, face the centerpiece—a photograph of the founder or chief instructor, a shrine in some instances—and execute a sharp bow from a standing position; this act is to be repeated each time there is a reason to leave and enter the dojo. As a sign of respect, this practice is also called for when visiting other aikido or non-aikido dojo. The first students arriving at the dojo are entrusted with the general clean-up before practice commences; the hall must be swept out and the mats either dry-mopped or swept also. No one is *ever* permitted to step onto the mats wearing street shoes or other footware. Socks are permitted, with the approval of the instructor, in the event of foot ailments or injuries. A student should not step on the mat barefooted when coming off the street in that manner. Once on the mats, students and instructors must execute a bow from a kneeling position, again toward the centerpiece. It should be repeated each time one steps on or off the mat for some reason.

In the event a student is tardy, he must, after changing into his practice uniform, officially approach the instructor in charge. He will execute a standing bow, state his reasons for being late, and, upon being acknowledged, will bow again and resume his proper position in the class. The bow is an important ritual under the teachings of budo. For example, should a student be corrected by the instructor, he is required to bow before and after the assistance, accompanied by a loud verbal *"Ohss."* This vocal term signifies understanding, acknowledgement, and at times, a greeting or goodbye.

When the class convenes for practice, the students form a line by seniority and assume a seiza position facing the instructor. The instructor and students should face the centerpiece of the dojo. The senior student (at the left of the centerpiece) calls out a sharp command, *"Rei"* (bow), and all bow in unison. The instructor then turns around to face the class, at which time the student again issues another sharp command, *"Sensei ni rei"* (bow to the instructor) and the instructor and students execute a mutual bow. Class then commences.

Opponents facing each other for the first time on the mat are expected to bow from a standing position at the outset, and again when breaking off the assigned workouts. If an attacker should accidently injure the defender, perhaps due to the inability of the person to move out in time, the attacker is expected to bow while apologizing—*"Sumimasen"* (excuse me). In budo, all activities begin and end with courteous behavior and consideration for one another; thus, the emphasis on the traditional Japanese practice of bowing.

Fingernails should be kept neatly trimmed at all times to prevent injuries. Women, in particular, often sustain painful tearing of their nails if kept unusually long.

Budo courtesies in Keijutsukai Aikido dictate that undivided attention be given to the instructor during class, and practice pursued in a serious vein. Students are not permitted to break off practice without first obtaining approval of the instructor. By the same token, sitting around "Indian style" or sprawled out on the mats during breaks is not allowed; the seiza position is maintained throughout the class period.

Instructors should be addressed as "Tanaka Sensei," rather than the Westernized version of "Sensei Tanaka." The former is the correct usage, with the surname preceding the honorific title. This applies to the other budo arts of Japanese origin as well.

CONDITIONING EXERCISES

This chapter deals with a number of routine exercises generally performed at the beginning of each class under the supervision of the instructor (or designated assistant) who calls out the specific exercise and counts aloud the repetitions ("one, two," etc.). A new student should not be expected to keep up with the rest of the group but should be permitted to do each exercise at his own pace for about a month or two to prevent painful muscular strains.

These exercises consist of special limbering and strengthening movements designed to better prepare the student for performing Keijutsukai Aikido techniques; they improve muscle coordination and flexibility as well as balance. Many are quite different in approach from that of other aikido schools. After you become familiar with the exercises, combined they should take no more than 30 minutes to complete before regular Keijutsukai training begins.

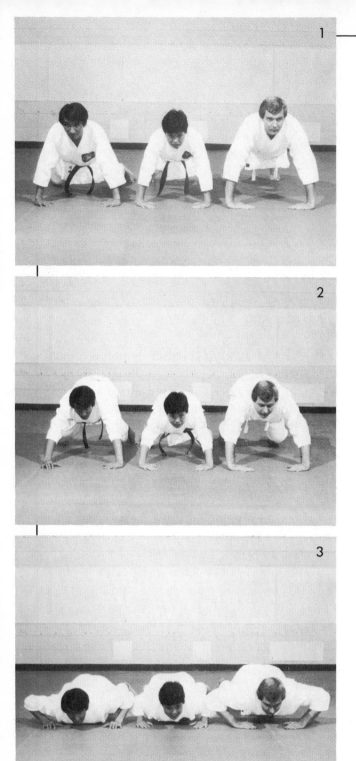

ROTATION PUSH-UPS

(1) Your body is raised on the palms and toes, legs slightly apart and arms spread at a comfortable distance. Your back should be horizontal and your eyes looking straight ahead. (2) Slowly push back, keeping your arms fully extended and maintaining a straight back throughout. (A taller person may find that the knees may touch the floor, but try to place only minimal weight on the knees.) (3&4) Bend your elbows and slowly move your body forward with your chest lightly brushing the floor. Extend your elbows again and raise your body up and out,

straightening the knees. Repeat. (At the outset, do only half a dozen repetitions maximum. Then gradually increase the total to 15 repetitions.) (5) After completing the first half of the rotation push-ups, continue to extend your body forward, back straight and elbows locked, until your shoulders project forward beyond your palms (which are flat on the mat). Don't let your abdomen sag. (6) Lower your body to the floor and gradually return to your starting position (keep your eyes looking ahead and your back rigid). Repeat.

1

SPRINGING PUSH-UPS

(1) Assume the conventional push-up position, eyes front and back straight. (2) Lower your body toward the mat and hold, but do not let your chest touch the mat. (3) Spring into the air with a quick upward thrust, keeping your body as uniform as possible. (4) Drop down into the lowered position of step #2 without touching your chest to the mat. Repeat. (*Note:* Do not attempt this exercise until your body is conditioned, then increase the repetitions gradually.)

ROLLBACKS

(1) Assume a seated position on the mat as shown, keeping your feet together and hands at your sides. (2) Roll backward until you place your toes on the mat behind you. Keep your knees extended by pushing against your heels. Return to your starting position and repeat. *Gradually* work up to ten repetitions. Do this exercise slowly at first, paying careful attention to the neck area (which can be injured easily if you are out of shape). To increase the difficulty of this exercise, follow a set of ten rollbacks with five to ten "holds," maintaining position #2 for a slow count of ten before returning to the seated position.

ABDOMINAL *(Fukin)*

Lie on your back and relax completely. Lift your feet, heels together, approximately six inches off the mat. Then, using your abdominal muscles only, lift both shoulders off the mat, chin tucked into the chest. Keep your legs fully extended, pushing your heels out and curling your toes in. If you do not feel a strong pull along your Achilles tendon, you are not maintaining the correct leg position. This exercise is beneficial to the abdominal muscles and the lower back, as well as the ankles and knees. Keep your shoulders relaxed—do not tense them at any time. Your hands must be kept free and extended—do not grip your thighs or pants. Hold this position for a slow count of ten. Ultimately, you should be able to maintain this position for a slow count of 30. Then lower your body entirely for a moment, then repeat for another count of 30. Do not attempt to hold a count of 30 in the early stages of your training—correct body position is more important here.

SQUAT JUMPS

(1) Assume a squat position on your toes, back and shoulders straight and your eyes straight ahead. Your hands should be placed as shown. (2) On an audible count of "one, two, three," execute three low jumps in preparation for one high jump. (3) At the audible command, "Jump!" spring into the air completely and kick both heels against your buttocks at the highest point. Land in the position in step #1. Balance will be difficult at first, especially when landing. Practice will keep you from inclining forward each time you drop back on the mat. Ten repetitions should be your goal after a few months.

Caution: Students who have experienced previous knee or ankle injuries and/or problems should not perform this exercise. Instead, substitute a regular "up-down" squat by holding onto a gymnasium handrail or the back of a chair to prevent unnecessary weight from pressuring your leg joints. Keep your back straight and squat slowly on your toes, maintaining your balance. Five to ten repetitions should be possible with practice.

BODY STRETCH

(1) Start in a prone position, chest resting on the mat and your feet propped up on your toes. Your body should be relaxed. (2) Push up with your arms, gradually flexing your back. Lift your head as well, turning your face up as far as it will comfortably go, flexing your neck muscles. Your thighs should still be on the mat. (3) Gently twist toward the left side, using your hips, and turning your face to the left as well. Keep your arms fully extended. (4) Now gently twist to your right side. (5) Push your body straight back and attempt to sit back on your heels. Stretch comfortably, with your back straight and your eyes looking forward. Do not bend your elbows. Strive to lower your chest to the mat and try to have your forearms placed flat on the mat as you push back. Repeat ten times.

DUCK WALK

(1) Assume a squat position on the mat, balancing on your toes only and keeping your arms clasped behind your neck. Keep your back and shoulders vertical by pushing your elbows out to your sides. (2) Step forward with your left foot, taking care not to let your right knee touch the mat. (3) Step forward with your right foot, keeping your left knee from touching the mat. (4) Repeat,

walking an entire lap around the dojo. Do not let your upper body incline forward during this exercise. If the mat area is very small, do more than one lap.

Caution: As with the squat jump exercise, persons who have experienced knee and ankle problems and/or injuries should refrain from doing this exercise.

LEG AND BACK STRETCH

(1) Assume a seated position on the mat as shown, toes curled in. (2) Bend forward slowly, striving to touch your chest to your knees/thighs. Do not flex or bend your knees. Your toes must be curled in to stretch the Achilles tendon. (3) Return to your starting position, then spread your legs wide apart and stretch down to your left ankle, trying to touch your chest to your thigh. Your eyes should be looking at a point in front of your toes. (4) Return to your starting position and stretch forward, trying to

lower your chest to the mat if possible. Do not let your knees buckle, and keep your toes pulled inward. (5) Return to the starting position and stretch toward your right ankle. Do not expect to reach these positions right away or very easily. Work up to ten repetitions, repeating the cycle in the same order. Once you are able to stretch without strain, have a partner gently push you from behind (palms on your lower back) to increase the stretch. Do not push on the shoulder blades.

FRONT AND BACK BENDS

(1) Stand with your feet about shoulder width apart, body relaxed. (2) Keeping your knees locked, bend over and touch the mat at a point just in front of your body, palms flat on the mat. From this position, bounce gently up and down (from the hips). (3) Raising your palms off the mat a few inches, utilize the same springing action to touch the mat just in front of your toes. (4) Now reach deeply between your legs and touch your fingers to the mat, and

bounce gently. The knees should remain locked. (5) Now return to your standing position and bend backward slowly, hands on hips and head bent back. Let your knees bend naturally to assist your balance. Perform the same gentle bounce backward as with the front bends. Do not tense your shoulder or use your hands on your hips to keep your body from losing its balance; bend just enough to keep your balance comfortably. Repeat ten times.

SIDE BENDS

(1) From a relaxed standing position, bend your body sideways to your left, and attempt to touch the outside of your left ankle with your left hand. Do not bend your knees and do not let your body lean forward. Your right arm is brought over your head naturally. Use your hips like a set of springs to gently touch the ankle twice. (2) Repeat on your right side. Do ten repetitions on each side.

NECK ROTATIONS

(1) Stand with your heels together and hands at your sides. Drop your head forward, chin touching your chest. Keep the rest of your body completely relaxed. (2) Turn your head to the left, taking care not to raise your left shoulder up to your face or ear. (3) Continue to circle your head to the rear, keeping your body straight and relaxed throughout. (4) Continue until your right ear is near your right shoulder. Repeat. After five complete repetitions, repeat the cycle in the opposite direction.

KNEE WALK *(Shikko)*

This exercise illustrates the correct way of moving from a semi-kneeling position. (1) Assume a kneeling position, with your buttocks resting on your upturned heels and your back and shoulders maintained vertically. Your feet should be propped up on your toes, and your eyes should look straight ahead. (2) Raise your right knee and pivot forward at a 45-degree angle, using your left knee as the pivotal point. Keep your body straight as possible. (3) Place your right knee on the mat and simultaneously bring your left and right heels together again. Your lead-

ing knee should now be pointed forward in the direction you are traveling. Do not allow the knee to turn in. (4) As your right knee touches the mat, pivot your entire body to your right as you bring your left knee off the mat pointed forward (your right knee is now the pivotal point). (5) Bring your left knee onto the mat and your heels together. Execute step #2 and repeat. Your balance and hip power will improve with these steps. Several laps around the dojo area are recommended to improve strength as well.

KNEELING, BOWING AND FORM EXERCISES

The normal aikido stance is descended from traditional Japanese sword-wielding forms, and many of the techniques closely resemble the sword handling movements of old. The original techniques, in fact, were patterned after these movements, such as the pure forms of jujitsu. Thus, one who is well versed in the intricate motions of *aiki* is generally quite adept in the handling of the sword.

Bowing to an opponent(s) or your instructor is both a dojo courtesy and an integral part of Japanese tradition, analogous to shaking hands. The budo type of bowing, however, is slightly different from that performed every day by the Japanese people. Bowing in the dojo signifies that training begins and ends with mutual respect and courtesy for your associates; it is also done whenever your instructor corrects an error on your part.

Though there are a number of form exercises routinely covered in Keiju-tsukai Aikido training, limited space makes it impractical to explain them all here. A few representative examples have been chosen which should be quite helpful to your training. Some of these forms may appear similar to that of other schools, but the emphasis and explanations of each are completely different.

These form exercises reinforce one of the primary requirements of Keiju-tsukai Aikido; that of dealing with your natural body flow and becoming compatible with the moves of an opponent through normal reflex action. They will serve to train your body—with your hips at the core—to react naturally and to learn to become completely relaxed in mind and body over a few months of steady practice.

BASIC STANCE AND KNEELING

(1) Assume a relaxed attention stance, heels together with your feet at a 45-degree angle and your hands at your sides. (2) Step forward with the right heel leading (imagine that the small of your back has been nudged forward), keeping your back and shoulders straight to center your weight (do *not* let your upper body tilt to the rear, shifting your center of gravity). Position your hands as illustrated, fingers extended and centered in front of your chest. Your eyes should always look straight into the eyes of your opponent. (3) Gradually lower your left knee to the mat while keeping your upper body straight and hands fixed. (4) Bring your right knee down, with your buttocks resting on your heels (see inset 4A) and your hands folded over your thighs. (5) This is the final kneeling position *(seiza)*, with the buttocks resting upon the calves as well as your heels. (6) In returning to an upright stance, the hands are again extended and the right foot is planted, heel next to your left knee. (7) Keeping your back and shoulders straight, rise to the standing position, known as the *migi hanmi* (right half-body position). (8) Bring your right foot alongside your left, assuming your original stance.

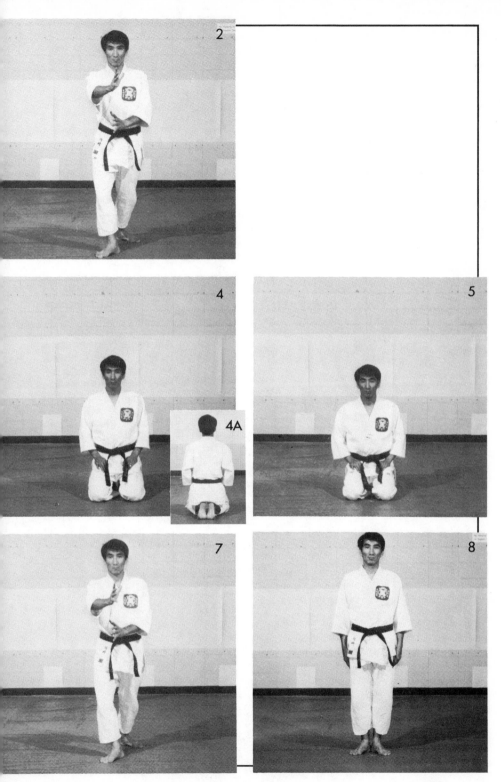

BOWING COURTESY
(Kneeling)

(1) Assume the kneeling position *(seiza)* and reach out with your left hand and place it palm down on the mat just in front of your left knee. (2) Follow immediately with your right hand in the same fashion, eyes looking straight ahead. Your thumbs and index fingers should form a triangle on the mat. (3) Maintaining a straight back and eyes front, lower the upper half of your body, bending the elbows naturally (almost touching the mat). If possible, the buttocks should still be resting on the heels (if not, then raised minimally). *Note:* Do *not* bob up and down, utilizing your head and neck.

BOWING COURTESY
(Standing)

(1) Stand and face your partner, heels touching and your feet angled at 45 degrees. Keep your back straight and your hands alongside your gi pants at all times. (2) Execute a sharp bow from the waist (hips) only and continue looking at your partner's eyes. (3) Straighten up again, sharply.

BODY MOVEMENT TRAINING
(Front and Rear)

(1) Assume a relaxed attention stance. (2) Step forward into a migi hanmi. (3) Using your hips and lower back, step forward *deeply* with your right foot (your left foot should pull up slightly to compensate for your overall balance), simultaneously raising your arms into the position shown. Drop your hips as low as possible. Push up and out with your elbows, wrists turned in slightly so that your right thumb points at your forehead and your left thumb at your

3

4

nose. Your hands should be approximately 12 inches away from your face. (4) Return to position #2, the migi hanmi. Repeat a minimum of five times for each side, reversing your stance for the left side. Perform this on a count of *ichi* (one: step out to the front) and *ni* (two: return to original position). Concentrate on moving from the small of the back, rather than initiating the move by stepping out first with the foot.

BODY MOVEMENT TRAINING
(Front and Rear Pivotals)

(1) Assume a migi hanmi position (the demonstrators here are facing in opposite directions to show the correct position throughout this exercise from both front and rear views). (2) Moving on the balls of your feet (never your heels), begin pivoting to your left using your hips and shifting approximately 60 percent of your weight onto your left foot. Simultaneously, begin to extend your leading hand forward (the same as your leading foot; in this case, your left) and your other hand (your right) down at your side. (3) At 180 degrees, your left hand should be in front

with your left wrist centered in front- of your chest. Your right hand is now completely down at your side, fingers extended. (4) Pivot your body back the way it came and step forward deeply with your right foot, extending the arms as shown (refer to position #3 in the previous exercise). This completes one cycle. Repeat five times and then reverse your stance and pivot to the right five times. At the command *yoi* (prepare), pivot. At the command *kamae* (stance), assume the migi hanmi position from position #4.

BODY MOVEMENT TRAINING
(Modified Front Pivotal)

(1) Assume the migi hanmi position. (2) Using your hips and lower back, move your left foot forward (note the position of your arms). (3) Continue moving your left foot smoothly out into a 45-degree stance (steps 2 and 3 should be executed in one continuous motion). Extend your left arm fully in the same direction as your left foot, with your palm up and held slightly above your head. Keep your shoulders relaxed. Approximately 60 percent of your weight should be on your left foot, with your upper torso inclined slightly forward. This is a *hidari* (left) hanmi position. (4&5) Return to your initial position in one smooth motion. Use a count of "ichi" to go forward and "ni" to return. Repeat a minimum of five times, then repeat on the opposite side.

BODY MOVEMENT TRAINING
(Modified Rear Pivotal)

Following the previous exercise, remain (1) in the migi hanmi stance in preparation for the second half of this modified set. (2) Again concentrating on your lower back and hips, pivot sharply (without wobbling) to your left on the ball of your right foot and extend your arms, palms up. Your left foot should make a very wide arc when pivoting to the rear to enable your hips to lower correctly. (3) At the end of your pivot, your left foot should be behind your right

in a migi hanmi stance. Instead of a complete 180-degree turn, you are at a 45-degree angle from a complete rear position. Your arms are extended in slightly different positions: your right arm in this example extends out in a straight path from your shoulder, while your left hand is at chest level. (4&5) Pivot back into your original position, your left foot traveling the same path as before. Repeat five times, then execute the pivotal in the opposite direction.

BASIC DIRECTIONAL THROWS
(Shiho Nage)

Beginning with this chapter, some basic techniques in Keijutsukai Aikido will be demonstrated. To simplify understanding of the mechanics involved, a few commonly practiced techniques (found in the majority of aikido schools) have been chosen. Though the techniques may appear to be the same as taught elsewhere, a careful study of the explanations will quickly reveal the differences in Keijutsukai training.

A word of advice: strength, per se, is *never* applied to *force* a technique upon the receiver or opponent; the lowered, well-balanced position of your hips and lower back should be considered the primary controlling factor, as we have so often described in the previous exercises. Your legs and arms should move naturally, *after your hips initiate the directional movements.*

Practice with caution at all times to prevent any accidental injuries to your partner, and immediately release or stop any movement when resistance is felt—you may be applying a technique improperly. Start over again, and perform the motions slowly. Speed will come naturally once your body is smoothly coordinated.

The *shiho nage* is a popular aikido technique, often referred to as the "four corners" throw. It should be interpreted as the "directional" throw, since it may be executed in any direction along the lines of a compass or circle, and not just in four directions. In the past, execution of the shiho nage depended on the non-resistance or patterned movement of your "opponent," either from a stationary position or prescribed striking action. It is highly doubtful, however, that the shiho nage as taught by such methods would be very effective in an actual confrontation, when your attacker may not move in the "prescribed" fashion.

The shiho nage is often executed—improperly—by utilizing pure strength instead of movement along the lines of natural flow. These deficiencies result when there is no proper understanding or adequate explanation of the correct principles involved.

In this section, and with the classification forms that follow, both frontal *(omote)* and reversal *(ura)* movements are demonstrated. As a general rule, frontal techniques are employed when the defender is forced to move ahead due to the pulling force of his opponent. The defender is merely going with the flow. The reversal techniques are employed when one is forced back by the momentum of an attacker; in both cases, the identical techniques are employed.

FRONT DIRECTIONAL THROW
(Omote Waza)

From a migi hanmi stance, (1) your opponent (*uke,* on the right) grabs your left wrist with his right hand and pulls slightly. Execute an *atemi* or strike (in this case, a backfist) to your opponent's face as a diversionary tactic (in practice, your partner should shield his face by placing his left hand and forearm up, palm out). Simultaneously, extend the fingers of your left hand and begin to step out to your opponent's left. (2) Grip your opponent's right wrist lightly with your right hand and step out deeply to your right (approximately 45 degrees) while extending both arms out in a fixed position, near chest

level. (3) Keeping your arms extended forward, continue to step out with your left foot (lead with your heel, not your toes, to help keep your hips squared and your body balanced). Your hands should be about face level, with your elbows bent slightly but locked firmly (they must not be permitted to flex throughout the technique). (4) Pivot to your right on the balls of your feet, letting your hips do the work to maintain your lowered, balanced position when moving. *Keep your upper left arm flush against your opponent's arm* as your right hand continues to

Continued on next page

5

6

grip his right wrist. (5) As your hips shift from left to right, execute a smooth lifting motion with your left elbow and upper arm, upsetting your opponent's balance and causing him to "roll" along your back. When executed properly, your hands will be at or near your forehead, palms out, and arms still forming a circle. *Under no circumstances* should you raise or pull your arms high over your head, for this will immediately halt the normal flow of leverage, and strength will be required to complete this throw. (6) As you complete your pivot (changing direction 180 degrees) extend your arms out and down, curling your opponent's wrist inward at the same time. Your right thumb and fingers should now have a firm grip on your opponent's wrist and hand, and with a slight inward pressure toward his right shoulder, he will lose his balance. (7) In practice, your partner could take a bad fall at this point. You should delay momentarily to allow your partner to execute a painless fall to his left side and letting his knees bend naturally, slapping the mat sharply with his left arm/palm. You must step forward slightly as your partner falls, bringing your right foot and body parallel to his. Your left knee is next to your right heel. (8) Keep your back straight and your right arm fixed, firmly holding down your opponent's wrist. Use a left hand blade strike *(tegatana)* to his face to subdue him. Again, your partner should block this atemi with his free hand.

REVERSE DIRECTIONAL THROW
(Ura Waza)

(1) You and your partner assume a *gyaku hanmi* (counter positions: left stance vs. right stance) and your partner grabs your left wrist with his right hand. (2) Extend the fingers of your left hand and move your left arm out, stepping out slightly to your left. Simultaneously, execute an atemi to your opponent's face (your partner should block as before). (3) Using your hips, pivot 180 degrees to your right by stepping with your right foot in a wide arc, transferring your weight from left to right. This backward

turn will bring you alongside your opponent, your left shoulder to his right shoulder. Use your right hand to lightly grab your opponent's right wrist and extend your arms out (hands at face level) into a fixed position, elbows bent slightly and arms forming a rough circle. Your left arm should be flush against your opponent's right arm. (4) As your hips shift from left to right (initiating another 180-degree turn), execute a smooth lifting motion with your left elbow and upper arm, upsetting your opponent's balance

Continued on next page

(5) and causing him to "roll" along your back. When executed properly, your hands will be at or near your forehead, palms out, and arms still formed in a circle. *Under no circumstances* should you raise or pull your arms high over your head, for this will immediately halt the normal flow of leverage (and may injure your partner). (6) Before the actual drop, this is where both partners should be positioned. You

should be in the migi hanmi, with arms extended (elbows and wrists still locked) and lowered, bringing your opponent's wrist in toward his right shoulder. (7) Step forward to line your body up with your opponent's as he falls. (Remember, in practice, allow your partner to fall correctly, slapping the mat with his left arm/palm.) (8) Execute an atemi to your opponent's face.

CLASSIFICATION FORMS

In this chapter we will cover the four basic classification forms taught by various aikido schools. These techniques lay the groundwork for much of the theory behind proper execution (and understanding) of Keijutsukai Aikido. These techniques must be practiced diligently for months with different partners so a student can get a feel of using his entire body (and not just his arms and hands) to "fit in" with his opponent and render that opponent's attack harmless.

Working with different partners helps a student learn to execute the same technique properly, though each opponent is different and may respond less readily to an application. With time the student will learn to feel these differences in response and adapt. Above all, take your time in learning these classification forms. The self-defense applications illustrated later on will be impossible to follow or execute if you do not have a thorough understanding of the following techniques.

FIRST CLASSIFICATION FORM
(Ikkajyo Kihon Waza)

This is the first of four well-known classification forms taught in aikido under various schools and methods. It is often shortened to *"ikkyo"* by some schools. This technique (both frontal and reversal) employs the use and practice of the form exercises covered earlier. It is essentially a block and takedown technique.

SHOMEN UCHI IKKAJYO
Omote (Frontal)
—Against Strike—

(1) Assume a normal position of attention, eyes focused on each other. (2) Move forward into the migi hanmi stance, extending your arms and fingers as shown and maintaining eye contact. (3) Your opponent (on the left) attempts a right overhead strike. Raise both your arms, palms out, and execute a double forearm block (4) using your hips to power the block and to maintain your forward momentum. Be sure your palms face out so that you block with the soft, inner portion of your forearms to prevent a painful bruise or fracture. (5) Without stopping, slide

your right hand (palm down) along the top of your opponent's forearm, lightly gripping the top of his hand while simultaneously sliding your left hand (palm up) to his elbow. When you push up against his elbow it will rotate forward naturally. Snap your hips sharply to the right, pivoting on the ball of your right foot. Keep your arms fully extended (do *not* bend your elbows) and *guide* his right arm down using your right hand. (6) The firm pressure against his elbow in conjunction with your hip movement will give you the natural leverage to upset

Continued on next page

his forward balance. (7&8) Stepping approximately 45 degrees to the right, move forward as your opponent falls, to compensate for the possible loss of balance if you are pulled forward. Keep your back as straight as possible, look straight ahead and keep your arms extended out away from your body. Always move from the hips and lower back! (9) Drop to your left knee parallel to your opponent's fallen body (your knee should be placed snugly against his right armpit) and make sure your left foot is up on the toes. (10) Drop to your right knee, placing the knee against your oppo-

nent's wrist joint. Your opponent's prone position and right arm should form a 90-degree angle if you have executed the technique correctly. Cup your left palm over the back of his right elbow and keep a firm grip on his wrist, holding it to the mat. Maintain a straight back; eyes forward. Press your weight down gradually onto the back of his elbow. When your partner slaps the mat, immediately release the hold. (11&12) Upon release, both men should separate, assuming first the half-kneeling position, eyes meeting, and then the migi hanmi posture, arms extended.

SHOMEN UCHI IKKAJYO
Ura (Reversal)

—Against Strike—

(1) Assume the *gyaku hanmi* (counter stance), arms extended. (2) Your opponent (on the right) attempts a left overhead strike, which you block with both arms, palms out, your left palm against his forearm and your right palm at or near his elbow. Let's assume for this exercise that your opponent comes in much stronger and faster than in the previous case, so that you are forced into a defensive response and only momentarily catch (but not stop) the blow. (3) *At the instant* of contact with your attacker's arm, pivot on the ball of your right foot to the your left, stepping back in a wide arc with your left foot (always moving from the hips) and keeping your arms extended, elbows locked to assist his own forward momentum. (4) Continue pivoting. Note the lowered hips and erect posture (the migi hanmi stance). Your elbows are locked, and you should have a firm grip on your opponent's wrist while maintaining a steady downward pressure on his elbow to (5&6) take your opponent down. Remember: *do not pull* his wrist and arm around. Your arms only guide his fall as your hips pivot. Immediately release your hold if you encounter any difficulty guiding your partner down to the mat. It means you are not properly balanced and coordinated. (7) When you drop to the mat, make sure your left knee is against his wrist, and your right knee against his armpit (it does not matter which knee is positioned first; normally, the knee nearest the mat is dropped first). Apply pressure to the elbow joint as in the previous technique. (8&9) Release the lock and spring up into the half-kneeling position, then return to your initial ready position.

SECOND CLASSIFICATION FORM
(Nikajyo Kihon Waza)

The *nikajyo waza* employs an unusual type of wristlock which can either be used to immobilize or throw an opponent. Although the basic form is used against a grasping attack, it is not limited to that situation. It may be used for a number of striking attacks as well. These applications will become more apparent as the student practices and learns to fit in with the movements of his adversary.

The nikajyo is also a technique that has caused many painful injuries over the years. This lock should never be "twisted" to create pain; it is applied *against* and *into* the wrist joint. If lingering pain results for hours or days, it means the lock was forced, aggressively wrenching the wrist—both unnecessary and incorrect.

KATATE MOCHI NIKAJYO
Omote (Frontal)
—Against Grab—

From the migi hanmi stance, (1) your opponent (on the right) grasps your right wrist with his left hand. (2) Immediately execute a backfist strike *(uraken)* to your opponent's face, simultaneously extending your right arm and fingers out to your side at waist level (your partner blocks your strike with his right forearm). (3) In a smooth continuous motion, step out with your right foot and face your opponent at a 45-degree angle, bringing your extended right arm up to shoulder height. (4&5) Without stopping, move back toward your original direction and stance (first your left foot, then your right foot still in the leading position) as you circle your right palm over your opponent's left wrist and grasp his forearm firmly. At the same time, cover your opponent's left hand with your left hand to "capture" it. Notice that your oppo-

nent's left arm forms a rough 90-degree angle at the elbow. Your arms should be approximately shoulder height; this is the correct position just prior to applying the wristlock. Your right index finger and thumb should be circling the opponent's wrist joint and your left hand grips the outer portion of his left hand (refer to close-up on pages 92-93). (6) With your wrist, elbow and shoulder joints firmly fixed in a rough circular position, move forward (using your lower back and hips) and exert a very light pressure out and down on your opponent's wrist, forcing him to drop to his knee. You are turning his wrist out and up, using your right index finger and left index finger to apply downward pressure onto the wrist joint. You do not *twist* the captive wrist! Your hips will give you all the leverage you need to create excruciating pain.

Continued on next page

(7) At the moment your opponent drops, immediately slide your right palm behind his elbow and step out to your left (leading with your left heel). Extend your arms and maintain pressure on his elbow. (8&9) Move forward to take your opponent down (don't push or turn his arm) and keep a firm grip on his wrist. Position your right knee next to his armpit. (10) Pivot slightly to face your opponent, cradling his left arm in the crook of your

10

11

right elbow. (11) Reach over with your right hand and grip your gi on the left side, trapping your opponent's arm, and place your left hand (palm up) against the back of his elbow. (12) The *kime waza* is executed by pivoting on your right knee to your left, pivoting from your hips and not your shoulders. Maintain this pressure until your partner slaps the mat, then rise as set forth in the previous exercises.

12

Refer to photographs #4-6 on page 89

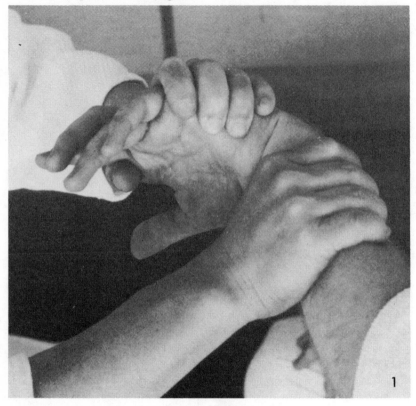

NIKAJYO WAZA (Close-Up)

Keeping your arms slightly circled and locked at the elbows, you apply the nikajyo lock in the following manner: (1) Use the four fingers on your left hand (in this case) to grip the fleshy outer portion of your partner's hand. Your partner's wrist should be turned up and out to its maximum natural stopping point (do not force beyond this point!) and your right knuckles should be directly over his wrist. Your thumb and fingers lightly, but firmly circle his forearm at the wrist joint. At this point, your partner should *not* be experiencing any pain, since his captive wrist and forearm are

Refer to photographs #4-6 on page 89

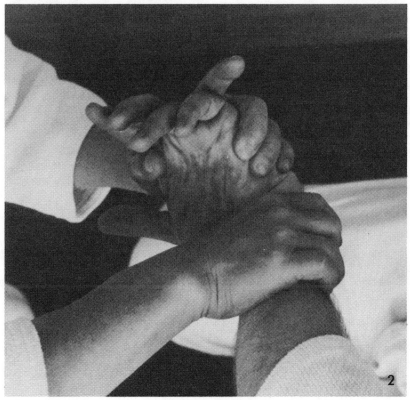

not being twisted or wrenched. Use your lower back and hips to initiate a forward move and exert a very light pressure (2) out and down with your right index finger and your left little finger. You are applying pressure to his wrist joint. The natural leverage and weight of your body will force your partner to drop in excruciating pain. Do not lift your hands up over your head and snap or twist downward onto your partner's wrist.

KATATE MOCHI NIKAJYO
Ura (Reversal)

—Against Grab—

(1) Assume the *gyaku han-mi* (left vs. right) counter stance. Your opponent (on the left) grabs your left wrist with his right hand and pushes. (2) Direct a backfist to your opponent's face (which he blocks) while extending your left arm out to your left side, stepping out with your left foot in the same direction so that you now face your opponent from a 45-degree angle. (3) In a

smooth, continuous motion, rotate your left arm up to shoulder height and circle your left hand over his right wrist (4) while bringing your right hand up to cover his right hand, trapping it. You now apply the nikajyo lock as before (5) bringing your weight forward with your arms and elbows locked in position, forcing his right hand to rotate painfully upward

Continued on next page

and back until (6) he drops to the floor in pain. Follow your partner down until your hands are at hip level. (7) Execute a sharp pivoting movement by stepping back with your right foot in an arc (right foot behind left foot) into the hidari hanmi position, keeping your arms fixed and sliding your left palm behind your opponent's right elbow (see inset 7A). Do *not* pull with your right hand or bear down on his elbow joint; use your hands to guide your opponent around with your balance maintained with your hips and

lower body. Your swift pivot (8) will bring him down as you drop to your left knee. As with the frontal technique, (9) cradle your opponent's arm in the crook of your left elbow using your right hand, then (10) use your left hand to grip the right side of your gi and apply the hold by (11) shifting to your right. Keep your back straight and place a right tegatana against the back of his elbow. When he submits, rise as in the previous exercises and face each other again.

THIRD CLASSIFICATION FORM
(Sankajyo Kihon Waza)

The third classification form also deals with another type of wristlock which may be used to immobilize or throw an opponent. When applied correctly the *sankajyo* will turn the wrist around further than the *nikajyo* by making use of the normal physiological limitations of the wrist, elbow and shoulder joints, provided the defender executes certain moves to "fit in" with his opponent.

This section is only designed to show the basic sankajyo, though the form can be utilized against a number of grasping or striking attacks if need be. Here again, force must not be utilized to twist or wrench the wrist, only proper technique.

SHOMEN UCHI SANKAJYO
Omote (Frontal)
—Against Strike—

(1) From the migi hanmi stance, your opponent (on the left) attempts an overhead strike which you block with both palms, your left hand at his elbow and your right at his wrist. (2) Without pausing, using your hips for leverage, direct your force up and over your attacker's elbow to push him around. Keep your arms extended and firmly hold the outside of his right wrist in your right hand so he cannot free himself. Continue your forward momentum and execute a quick pivot (3) to your right, turning your opponent's wrist up and out. (The following pictures show a front view of the technique.) (4) Reach under your opponent's wrist with your left hand, gripping the fleshy part (below his little finger) securely and continue the turning pressure at his wrist joint. Do not release your right hand until your left hand has taken over the hold. (5) Now slide your right palm down until your right thumb hooks into the crook of his elbow, where you can easily press down on a nerve point that will control your opponent. Keep your arms extended and (6) step forward, dropping to your left knee as your opponent falls. Keep your back straight. (7&8) Changing your grip once again (here shown from a better angle), grab the captive wrist with your right hand and tuck his wrist (turning outward) into the left side of your chest, positioning a left tegatana behind his elbow. Your body and arms lock his arm securely. Release the lock when your partner signals.

SHOMEN UCHI SANKAJYO
Ura (Reversal)
—Against Strike—

(1) Assume the *gyaku hanmi* (left vs. right stance). In this situation, your opponent has the initiative and comes in strongly with an overhead strike. Block his arm momentarily, your right palm on his elbow and your left at his wrist. Immediately (2) pivot out with your left foot in a 180-degree arc, stepping back with your left foot as you guide his left arm down and then back up, complementing his momentum. Grasp his left hand with your left hand as soon as you block it, then bring his arm down as you push up firmly on his elbow. (3) Turn his wrist out so that his palm faces you. Bring your right hand down over your left to transfer your hold. You should use your hips and lower back to step forward. (4&5) Maintain your wristlock (see inset 4A) as you move forward, keeping your shoulder, elbow and wrist joints firmly locked. Step out and around your opponent and execute a sharp right turn on the ball of your foot. Do not let your shoulder become tense or you will limit the waza by substituting arm strength instead of hip strength! (6) Direct your opponent's captive arm out and down by pushing against his elbow with your left hand (thumb out) until he is on the mat (7), then reverse your left grip so that your thumb is in. Maintain the wrist hold and press your left thumb into the crook of his elbow. (8) Now cover the outer part of your opponent's left wrist with your left hand, transferring the lock without slackening the pressure. (9) His arm is now flush against your chest and a right tegatana is placed against the back of his elbow. Use your hips/lower back to steadily turn toward your left. Release the lock when your partner slaps the mat.

FOURTH CLASSIFICATION FORM
(Yonkajyo Kihon Waza)

The *yonkajyo* is another pressure point lock on an opponent's wrist. Properly applied, it can be an extremely painful technique to the recipient. It is also one of the most difficult ones among the basic classification forms for both novices and advanced belts. There is an erroneous idea that the lock consists of a tight gripping tactic and subsequent "flinging" of an opponent by directing pure force at the pressure point. Others use indiscriminate force against various portions of the inner wrist, in the mistaken belief that general pain is the objective. Both are incorrect. This section will attempt to demonstrate the yonkajyo application as it should be executed—not with hand or arm force—but with proper technique.

SHOMEN UCHI YONKAJYO
Omote (Frontal)

—Against Strike—

(1) Assume the migi hanmi against your opponent (on the right) and meet his attempted overhead strike with your raised palms, your right against his right wrist, your left at or near his right elbow. (2) Grip your opponent's right wrist and turn it palm up (toward you) while stepping out 45 degrees to your right. At the same time, push up and over with your left arm against his elbow. These moves should be executed in one smooth movement, using your hips for leverage to bring his right arm down. Your body must be inclined only slightly, and your arms firmly extended as you step forward (3) to bring your opponent to the mat. (4) Slide your left hand down to his wrist, keeping his palm face up and gripping the fleshy portion of his palm at the wrist joint. Keep your hips low. (5) Apply gradual pressure against the radius bone of his forearm (the point of contact is the base of your left index finger). Pressure is controlled using your hips, furnishing leverage through your extended left arm. Your left hand must be flush against his inner forearm or you will have to use pure force (incorrect!) to apply this pressure. (6&7) Continue to move forward 45 degrees to your left, maintaining this pressure as your opponent drops forward. (8) Taken from a different angle, this shows where you should position yourself to apply the final waza on your opponent. Place your opponent's arm into the crook of your left elbow and grip the opposite side of your gi with your left hand. Place a right tegatana against the back of his elbow, pressing his arm against your chest. (9) Turn toward your right (from the hips), keeping his arm held firmly vertical (same as the nikajyo lock).

SHOMEN UCHI YONKAJYO
Ura (Reversal)

—Against Strike—

(1) From a gyaku hanmi, your opponent (on the right) comes in powerfully with an overhead strike. Block as before, using your right palm against his right wrist, your left palm against his elbow. (2) Immediately arc your right foot back to your right (facing 90 degrees to the right of your previous position) while grasping your opponent's arm with both hands. Position yourself as close to your opponent as possible. (3) This photograph shows the technique from a new angle. Slide your left palm down on the inner side of his right forearm, gripping his wrist joint in the same manner as the previous yonkajyo (omote). (4) Using a firm hold with both hands, continue to pivot back and to your right (into a hidari hanmi) and direct strong pressure against your opponent's radius bone, (see inset 4A) lifting his arm up and forward. Your arm, elbow and wrist joints must be firmly locked and holding his arm so that it forms a rough 90-degree angle. (5) With a sudden forward and downward pressure, your opponent will fall to the mat. Keep your right hand encircling his wrist from the outside, turning it palm up. Your forward hip motion is applying pressure through your extended left arm. (6) Drop down onto your left knee and direct strong pressure against the contact point to make sure your opponent will not try to escape. (7) From another angle, you now pivot to face your opponent and cradle his captive right arm (8) in the crook of your left elbow, gripping your gi with your left hand and placing a right tegatana against the back of his right elbow (the nikajyo lock). Pivot slowly to your right (9) to apply. If his arm does not turn with you, you are not applying the lock effectively. Release the hold when your partner slaps the mat.

SELF-DEFENSE TECHNIQUES

In this chapter some of the practical self-defense aspects of Keijutsukai training are illustrated using, wherever possible, some of the basic techniques covered in previous chapters. Some of these defenses employ an extended or modified version of the basics, while others are deceptive in these photographed sequences—they are much more difficult than they appear, and should not be attempted by beginners. They are meant to offer just a few examples of aikido effectiveness in simulated assaults.

DEFENSE AGAINST REAR GRAB

(1) The opponent seizes your right wrist from behind and puts his left arm around your waist. (2&3) Step out with your left foot (moving from the hips) and rotate your right palm up as you pull your arm sharply forward and to your left. At the same time, reach down with your left hand and grab the outer portion of his left wrist. (4&5) Pivot quickly to your left as you free your right hand and pull his left hand firmly off your waist, maintaining your hold on his left hand. (6) Pivot behind him into a hidari hanmi, placing your right hand behind his elbow (pushing it up and over) and turning his left wrist palm up. (7&8) Move forward and pivot to your left, placing your right forearm and elbow against the back of his arm as you continue to turn his left wrist palm up and in toward his elbow. This will force your opponent down.

1

3

DEFENSE AGAINST REAR CHOKE

(1) Your opponent grabs you around the neck and seizes your right wrist. (2) Shift your body to the right and extend your right arm up (palm out) to shoulder level. (3) Reach across with your left hand and grab the outer fleshy portion of his right hand while pivoting sharply (4) to your left to free your right wrist. Push up on his right hand (5) and move forward (from the hips), keeping your left elbow and wrist rigid to exert upward pressure on his right arm. (6&7) Move around him applying the sankajyo ura waza, finishing with (8) a forward throw (do not attempt this last step without proper Keijutsukai supervision).

6

DEFENSE AGAINST REAR GRAB
(Two Opponents)

(1) Two men have grabbed your wrists from behind on either side. (2&3) Drop your hips and concentrate on one opponent (in this case, the right one). Pivoting to your right, raise your wrist up (palm out), bending at the elbow and then keeping the arm fixed as you shift to your right, forcing your opponent to let go and lose his balance. As your right wrist is freed, (4) immediately deliver an *uchi* (strike) to your other opponent's face. Use your captured left hand to reach outside of his left arm and grab his left wrist, pivoting quickly to your left to (5-8) execute an ikkajyo ura waza. With your second opponent on the ground, set the armlock (9) by trapping his left arm in the crook of your right elbow and press the back of his elbow against your chest with a left tegatana. (10) Pivot to your left until your opponent signals for you to release the lock.

DEFENSE AGAINST FRONT CHOKE

(1) Your opponent attempts a front choke. (2&3) Reach up with your left arm and press down quickly inside the attacker's right elbow as you pivot (using your hips) to your right. (4) Bring your right palm up outside his left arm and press up against the back of his elbow, (5) pivoting sharply 90 degrees to your left, keeping his right arm trapped against your abdomen with your left arm. Continue the pivot and the pressure against his elbow (6) until he is thrown forward (do not attempt this last step without Keijutsukai supervision).

2

3

5

6

1

2

3

DEFENSE AGAINST DOUBLE WRIST GRAB

(1) Your opponent seizes both your wrists in his hands. Begin pivoting to your right and (2) turn both your hands palm up as you raise your arms. Reach underneath your captured right hand with your left hand and grab the back of your opponent's left hand. (3) Pivot sharply until you are 90 degrees to your right, using your left hand to peel your opponent's hand from your right wrist. Move forward (4), pulling

his left hand out and down (his palm should face away from you). Your right hand is now free to hold the back of his left hand and trap it. (5&6) By continuing this pressure with your forward movement you will be able to throw your opponent (do not execute this last move without proper Keijutsukai supervision). The hips and lower back play an important role in this technique, an example of *kokyu* (compatibility).

DEFENSE AGAINST CLUB STRIKE

This technique employs the basic shiho nage against a club attack. (1) Facing your opponent in a migi hanmi, move forward strongly with your hips to step in and simultaneously (2) block his club strike with your left forearm and deliver a *uraken* (backfist) to his face. (3) Step out to your right as you reach over his right wrist and grab it from the outside with your left hand and grab the inner portion of his wrist with your right hand. (4) Draw his right arm up and out, keeping your arms, elbows and wrists firmly locked in a circular position, using only your lower body to move further to your right. (5) Pivot sharply back to your right as you bring his captive wrist over your head with your hands at forehead height. Remember to keep your arms rigid and let your body do the work. (6&7) Lower your arms as you step forward (now that your opponent's wrist is behind his right shoulder) and you will force your opponent to the ground. Drop your left knee to the mat as he falls while placing your right foot next to his right armpit. (8) This photograph shows the proper position for your body to be in to disarm your opponent, or to deliver a strike to his face.

ADVANCED SELF-DEFENSE TECHNIQUES

To the uninitiated, aikido techniques in action can appear deceptively simple. They are not. "Expert" demonstrations of aikido often promote a circus-like atmosphere as numerous opponents are hurled about with no apparent physical strain. The "secret" behind aikido techniques is not mystical power but a simple understanding of body mechanics, and especially, *kokyu* —the way of fitting in with the movements of an attacker.

A wide receiver in football or a great hitter in baseball has the perfect timing and coordination needed to meet a pass or a pitch at precisely the right moment. Any deviation from the precise moves needed will result in a dropped pass or a foul ball. Boxers, tennis players, hockey skaters—all great athletes have this indelible sense of where to be and when to move, usually faster than they can consciously think about it. All these athletes have some degree of kokyu. That is what is meant by the term.

The techniques in the following chapter demonstrate some advanced forms in Keijutsukai which could not be executed without this sense of kokyu. *Do not attempt to duplicate or practice the following techniques.* These can be extremely injurious to the receiver if not executed properly, and mere words and photographs cannot fully explain the techniques involved. These are only included for your enlightenment—so a beginner can see what to expect in Keijutsukai Aikido after many years of hard training.

KOKYU WAZA
(Compatibility Technique
Principle—Kneeling)

Even from a kneeling position, it is possible to use the principle of *kokyu ho* ("fitting in" with the moves of another) to overcome an opponent. (1) Your opponent grabs your wrists firmly in both his hands. (2) Turn your hands thumbs out so that your palms and forearms are face up. Your opponent should lurch forward if this movement is swift enough. (3) Keeping your arms slightly bent at the elbows, turn your thumbs inward as you lift

your arms simultaneously, lifting your opponent from the inside of his wrists. (4) By redirecting your opponent's balance, you can throw him (in this case) to the right side. All the movements have been done utilizing leverage from the lower body. If you use only your arms to "lift" your opponent, you would not succeed, especially if your opponent is much stronger. But proper leverage and timing can overcome size.

KOKYU NAGE
(Compatibility Throwing Technique)

(1) Your opponent has grabbed your wrists firmly. Utilizing only your hips and lower back for leverage, step forward (2) 45 degrees to your right with your left foot, simultaneously raising both your arms overhead (keeping the shoulder, elbow and wrist joints rigid and in a circular configuration). (3) Pivot sharply to your right on the balls of your feet, raising your

arms high and then (4) dropping onto your left knee. Keep your back straight and slightly inclined; a smooth extension of your arms forward in combination with the quick pivot and dropping of your weight will hurl your opponent in the direction he was originally facing. All these movements should flow together in one continuous motion.

KOKYU NAGE
(Variation #1)

This throw is exactly the same as the previous throw, with one exception. (1) Your opponent grabs both your wrists. Instead of raising both your arms overhead, (2) drop your left arm down to your side as you pivot 180 degrees, ex-

tending your right arm up, around and forward. (3) Drop your weight and extend your right arm, allowing your left arm to bend naturally at the elbow and behind your back. (4) Throw your opponent forward as you drop to your left knee.

KOKYU NAGE
(Variation #2)

(1) Your opponent grabs your right wrist with his left hand. (2) Immediately bring your right arm up firmly, forming a tegatana with your right hand and turning it in against your opponent's left wrist. (This applies pressure to his wrist joint.) This motion will hook your hand onto his wrist, forming a natural fit against the joint, without actually grabbing his wrist. Simultaneously, (3) step out and back in a wide arc with your left foot, pivoting

180 degrees on the ball of your right foot. Keep your right hand against the point of his wrist as you pivot and he will be off balance. (4) Extend your right arm forward (keeping it firmly rigid) and drop to your left knee (back straight) to throw your opponent forward. If you were to use only arm strength, ignoring the leverage in your lower body combined with timing, your opponent could not be thrown.

KOKYU NAGE
(Variation #3)

(1) Your opponent grabs your wrists firmly. (2) Using the natural leverage in your lower back and hips, raise your arms (again, your elbows bent slightly) and hook the outside portion of your wrists along the inside of his wrist joints. (3) As he raises up on his toes, move forward swiftly (leading with the hips) under-

neath his left arm and bring your arms down quickly (4) behind you, using your weight to transmit the leverage down your arms. As you drop to one knee, grab your opponent's wrists lightly as his arms go past. This guides his arms until you release (5) them, throwing him forward.

AIKI NAGE

(1) Two opponents hold your wrists on either side. (2) Drop back and lower your weight, simultaneously raising your arms back and outside their wrists in a circular motion until your hands are over your head. Keeping your arms firmly

fixed and slightly bent at the elbows, (3) drop to your left knee (in this case) when your opponents are off balance and bring your arms down and forward quickly. Both men (4) will be thrown forward.

NIKAJYO OMOTE WAZA
(Modified)

(1) Your opponent grabs your right wrist with his left hand. Move forward slightly and (2) twist your right tegatana outside of his wrist and hook it on top, applying pressure against his wrist joint and (3) lowering your weight. By covering his left hand with your left hand, you will trap his

hand on your wrist as your body applies the leverage, immobilizing him and dropping him to the ground (4) in pain. You must keep your hand firmly against the back of his wrist joint at all times, using your whole body to supply the leverage, never just your wrists or arms.

IKKAJYO OMOTE WAZA
(Modified)

As your opponent moves in with a downward knife thrust, (1) step in quickly and block his blow with your left hand (remember to use your whole body, not just your arm!) and simultaneously (2) reach up and across with your right hand and grasp the outside of his right wrist. (3) Pivot sharply to your right on the balls of both feet while positioning your left hand against the back of his right elbow. (4) Step out with your left foot in the direction of your opponent's left armpit, then drop your weight as you continue to pivot (5&6) to your right. By keeping your arms in a rigid circle you will hurl your attacker forward.

HIJI SHIME
(Elbow Lock)

When your opponent attempts a downward knife thrust, (1) step in and block his wrist with your left arm (using your whole body for momentum) and immediately execute a *uraken* (backfist) to his face (2) with your right hand (your partner should block this blow with his free hand in practice). (3) Slide your left hand underneath his forearm and bring your right hand up to grasp the outside portion of his wrist joint with both hands. Use both hands to (4) draw his captive arm across your chest, forcing his palm to turn up. Use your hips and pivot on the balls of your feet, locking his elbow and leaning your chest and left arm down onto his elbow joint. His arm must be keep flush against your body. (5) Lower your weight to take him to the ground.

KOTE GAESHI
(Outer Wristlock Throwing Technique)

(1) As your opponent threatens with a knife thrust, pivot away from his thrust (2) by stepping back with your right foot so that you are facing 90 degrees to the right of your position in step #1. Simultaneously deflect his right arm with your extended left arm, your left hand against the back of his wrist. (3) Step forward and firmly grip his wrist with your right hand and use your lower body to turn his wrist and hand in toward his body. (4) This angle shows how you should be facing your opponent as you pivot 180 degrees to your right. (5) The pressure against his wrist combined with your body pivot will throw him. (6) Place a right tegatana diagonally across the back of your opponent's elbow, maintaining steady pressure against the joint while stepping over his head (7) to turn his body face down (this photo shows the correct position after this move). (8) Align yourself along side your opponent's body and exert gradual pressure down upon his wrist, forcing him to release the knife in pain.

2

4

5

7

8

PIVOTAL THROW
(Nage)

(1) The defender is grasped by the wrists from behind by two opponents. (2&3) He steps out slightly (lowering his hips) and brings his arms up locked in circular fashion and pivots on the balls of his feet, drawing

the two men together and entwining them. (4) By stepping out, keeping his arms extended, he is able to drop both men simultaneously. (5) This shows a front view of the throw.

KOTE GAESHI
(Outer Wristlock Throw, Modified—Knife Slash)

(1) The attacker attempts a slash at the defender's midsection. (2) The defender pivots out with his right foot, lightly deflecting the attacker's forearm from the outside. Covering the attacker's knife hand (from the outside) with his deflecting hand, the defender immediately brings his right hand up, crossing his right thumb over his left, and pivots back in two movements until his back is almost flush against the attacker's abdomen. The covering pressure combined with the fast pivot will (3) cause the attacker to fall violently.

KOKYU
(Nerve Point Throwing Technique)

(1) The attacker grabs the defender's left wrist with his left hand. (2) By grasping the attacker's wrist firmly in his right hand, utilizing a special nerve point technique located on the wrist, the defender will rise up in pain, allowing a quick pivotal movement (3) to unbalance the attacker and throw him forward.

YOKO NAGE
(Side Arm Throw)

(1) The attacker has grabbed the defender by the lapels while seated. (2) The defender places his right forearm inside the crook of the attacker's left elbow and simultaneously pushes up with his left hand under the attacker's right elbow. By redirecting the attacker's force to the left side using a slight pivot of the hips (while seated) the defender (3) can throw his opponent to the right.

YOKO NAGE
(Side Outer Wrist Throw)

(1) The attacker grasps the defender's lapel with his left hand and directs a punch to the face with his right fist. (2) The defender moves in unison with his opponent's left hand grip, pivoting to his right as he lightly deflects the attacker's strike from the outside of his wrist. At the moment of deflection, the defender grasps the attacking wrist and holds it securely while pivoting, (3) flinging his opponent to the floor.

IRIMI NAGE
(Body Fitting Throw—Modified)

This technique is a modified *irimi nage.* (1) The attacker grasps the defender's lapel in his left hand. (2) The defender places his right hand against the back of the attacker's left elbow from the outside and pivots with his hips to direct pressure down and to the left. The attacker's elbow will be pushed up, causing him to lose his balance.

KOKYU ATEMI
(Compatibility Strike Forearm)

(1) As the attacker attempts to stab the defender, (2) the defender moves forward suddenly executing a throat strike with his right arm, meeting his attacker unexpectedly with split-second timing. The attacker is caught off guard, and his own momentum carries his body into the line of the defender's strike, causing him to be thrown up and over.

This technique should not be experimented with without proper training.

KNIFE DEFENSE
(Compatibility Elbow
Locking Throw)

(1) Your opponent threatens with a knife thrust. (2) As your opponent lunges forward, pivot sharply to your right, stepping back with your right foot (pivoting on your left foot) and lightly deflecting his attacking arm with your left hand. (3) Grab his right wrist immediately with your right hand and reposition your left arm underneath his elbow (do not slam your extended left arm against his elbow

joint). Simultaneously pivot to your right using the leverage in your lower back and hips. This will cause your opponent to "float" on his toes, unbalancing him and (4&5) allowing you to throw him forward using a steady, gradual pressure against his upper arm and elbow. The pressure is supplied through your extended left arm from your lower body as you pivot. *Do not attempt this technique as injuries may result.*

SIDE OUTER WRIST THROW—MODIFIED

(1&2) The attacker grabs the defender's lapel with his left hand and prepares to strike him with his right fist. The defender lightly deflects the blow toward his right as he moves slightly to the left, (3) then

grasps the attacker's right wrist from the outside with his own right hand. (4&5) By dropping to one knee and following through with a circular, forward motion, the attacker will be thrown.

AIKI NAGE

(1) The defender is grabbed by three opponents, one in front and two on either side. (2) The defender raises his arms up in circular fashion while stepping back slightly and lowering the hips and lower back.

(3&4) By pivoting quickly to the left and dropping his arms, the defender throws the opponent on his right against the remaining two men, entwining their arms and bodies for the throw.

SHIHO NAGE
(Directional Throw—
Seated, Modified)

(1) The attacker grabs the defender's left wrist. (2&3) The defender grasps the opponent's right wrist at a pressure point and turns his left wrist inward toward the right, redirecting the opponent's gripping force toward himself, immobilizing the opponent's wrist. (4-7) As the opponent rises up unbalanced due to the pain, the defender quickly pivots to his right while seated, executing a modified shiho nage, throwing his opponent.

KOKYU ATEMI
(Compatibility Strike—
Bokken or
Simulated Sword)

(1) The attacker prepares to step in and slash downward at the defender. (2) As the attacker moves in, the defender quickly steps out to the left to counter slash. This is shown merely as an example of the timing and *kokyu* required in the execution of advanced aikido.

KOKYU ATEMI
(Compatibility Strike—
Finger(s) Thrust)

(1) As the attacker prepares to slash downward at his opponent, (2) the defender steps out slightly and in before the attacker has a chance to finish his downward cut; the defender uses a finger thrust to the throat to stun his opponent. The opponent's own momentum takes him directly into the thrust.

JO OR BO DEFENSE
(Medium or Long Staff)

Many of the unarmed techniques used in advanced forms of aikido can be duplicated with the use of the *bo.* (1) The attacker (on the right) attempts to grasp the bo away from the defender. (2) The defender immediately steps out (using his hips for leverage) and extends the bo up and to the left. As a natural reflex, the opponent will not release his grip to prevent himself from falling. Once the attacker is unbalanced, (3&4) the defender follows through by dropping the bo downward in a circular manner and throwing the opponent to the rear.

APPENDIX I

EXAMINATION AND GRADING SYSTEM

Examinations in the official sense are not utilized at Keijutsukai dojo in Japan, since the students are under the personal supervision of the chief instructor at all times. Promotions are based on his evaluation of the students over a period of time, under normal practice conditions. However, a general promotional guideline is in effect, and all students are fully aware of the fact that certain requirements must be fulfilled in order to secure progressive promotions up to and including the dan levels.

Branches and affiliates outside of the chief instructor's personal supervision on a regular basis are subjected to examinations. The guidelines utilized by the headquarters for promotion are followed by them, with certain applicable changes appropriate in those areas. A copy of this guideline is included for those who are interested.

The Keijutsukai system of grading follows that of other schools, insofar as rankings are concerned. A new student is appointed to the tenth *kyu* (step), or initial white belt stage. Subsequently, the white belted student progresses through the ninth, eighth, seventh, sixth, and fifth kyu. At the fourth kyu, a green belt is awarded. From third, second and first kyu, a brown belt ranking is recognized. Then *shodan* (first degree black belt), *nidan* (second degree), etc. It should be mentioned that other aikido and non-aikido schools may observe a slightly different grading recognition, commencing at a different kyu and using various colors within the white belt level mentioned under the Keijutsukai—the shodan degree, however, is universal among the martial arts. A combination red and white or red belt is worn by those in the highest grades, generally the seventh, eighth, and ninth dans—the latter, an honorary rank which was bestowed by the late Uyeshiba; the highest in aikido from an official standpoint, and held by a few individuals who head their own schools of note which were sanctioned by him at that time. The head of a *recognized* system may also elect to wear a red belt, at his own discretion.

A specially designed, bilingual certificate is issued by the Keijutsukai from third kyu and up. However, a certificate may be awarded to those requesting same at the lower kyu level. A copy of the certificate is included in this section.

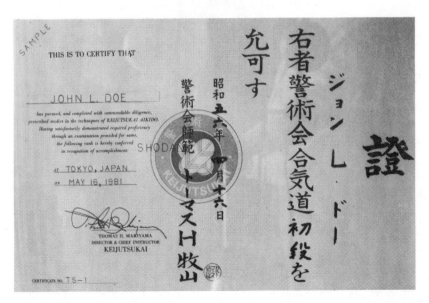

KEIJUTSUKAI AIKIDO PROMOTIONAL GUIDELINE

Tenth Kyu: A new student is appointed to this kyu, the initial step. The fundamentals, exercises, basic movements, falls, etc., will be taught at this stage.

Ninth Kyu: Students are promoted to this level after completing the basic requirements for the tenth kyu.

Eighth Kyu: At this level, students should be able to execute basic techniques without encountering too much difficulty. Simple variations (patterns) will be introduced. Example: Utilizing basic techniques when grasped by an opponent with one hand.

Seventh Kyu: Techniques taught at eight kyu can be employed with few errors. Additional expansion of defenses will be covered. Example: Techniques (simplified forms) employed when grasped by an opponent in different ways, but limited to a frontal approach toward the defender.

Sixth Kyu: Smooth execution of techniques taught at seventh and eighth kyu is expected of students promoted to this level. Various defenses against diversified holding tactics, strikes and punches will be emphasized at this point of training.

Fifth Kyu: A fairly controlled or fluid movement will be expected in executing techniques learned thus far, without relying too much on physical force. Further expansions and technique variations will be taught at this level of training to prepare the student for the next promotion.

Fourth Kyu: At this level (green belt), the student has demonstrated the ability to utilize different techniques and movements against simultaneous attacks from more than one opponent. Although considerable difficulties are still present, a student is able to react without committing serious errors. Movements of a static nature should become more natural. Obvious existing faults must be corrected at this stage. Students at fourth kyu will be required to correctly teach newer students as part of their own training (not all strong students make satisfactory instructors). Teaching others will definitely improve understanding of aikido techniques for the senior student, and tends to reveal faults not normally observed during his own training.

Third, Second, and First Kyu: Within this level (brown belt) promotions are based on a number of factors: general knowledge, dedication, sincerity, technical ability, teaching qualities, etc. Seniority is also an important criteria. Progressive promotions will depend upon the degree of proficiency demonstrated by the student during practice sessions through special examinations provided at the discretion of the Chief Instructor or his appointed representatives. Under normal circumstances, official certificates will be granted from third kyu through the Keijutsukai Headquarters.

Shodan: Promotion to this coveted goal is the ultimate objective of every student undergoing studies of Keijutsukai Aikido. The requirements are quite demanding and cannot truly be listed. It is safe to say that a number of intangible factors play an important role in the final determination of a shodan, along with satisfactory proficiency in all areas of techniques and related standards of conduct in the school. A potential shodan must also display the qualities of an instructor, able to conduct classes on his own. Higher promotions will be along similar lines, and at the final discretion of the chief instructor. In any event, the shodan ranking is much more difficult to attain through the Keijutsukai than from other aikido schools.

APPENDIX II

KEIJUTSU—SPECIALIZED TECHNIQUES
RELATING TO LAW ENFORCEMENT

The subject of self-defense training programs for law enforcement personnel has always been of primary concern to this author, since his early career in budo and law enforcement work within Japan and during the Korean outbreak. This section has been included to apprise those interested students involved with the subject of the practical implementation of martial arts programs in law enforcement training. It should be mentioned that this author's conclusions may reflect a strong and unfavorable picture; an indictment against the past and present approach to this type of training program by responsible authorities. However, these findings are based on personal experiences, interviews with active and inactive law enforcement personnel, and most importantly, the general consensus of top police executives concerned with the specific training. Equal emphasis must be placed on the area of unarmed self-defense, as well as other official subjects such as firearms, crime scene preservation, etc. The usual result of such discussions over the years was one of lukewarm interest at best, or apathy and complacency toward existing training methods. In all fairness, it should be made clear that the officers themselves, who were directly concerned at the grass roots, were highly responsive—being acutely aware of the shortcomings. However, the common obstacles—budgetary and lack of active support from above—has prevented progressive thinking and improvements in this important area. The following is a capsule opinion of faults (observed over the past 35 years), concerning the incorporation of budo defensive tactics in law enforcement. The United States and Japan have been singled out for this purpose, as representative examples best illustrating two extremes:

United States of America

The general trend has been to offer a set number of hours in unarmed self-defense, usually while an applicant is undergoing regular recruit training in police work. Normally, judo forms the basis of the self-defense programs, with a loose collection of theoretical ideas on Westernized jujitsu, karate, aikido, etc., that are tacked on as may be required to form a course with X number of hours. The result is an officer or agent who fits into the popular adage of a little knowledge being extremely dangerous.

Once assigned to regular enforcement duties, the individual rarely, if ever, attempts to continue training on his own time unless he is one of the few who personally enjoys the martial arts.

The majority of instructors teaching officers and agents are of lower black belt degrees in one or two of the arts. Though they may have experimented with other arts, they are not sufficiently trained to fully understand the mechanics of incorporating them into their own courses. Major emphasis is placed on their specialty, for example, judo. Unfortunately, the average student gains an improper impression that what he has "learned" in a few hours can be easily utilized in a practical situation.

The average officer or agent is insufficiently prepared to defend himself in a practical situation involving unarmed self-defense; thus, a routine arrest of a suspect can often result in a street brawl wherein the arresting officer is forced to resort to other forceful means—a baton, for example—which may prompt unfounded brutality charges. At other times, the arresting officer may come out second best, unless he has assistance.

Instructors generally fall under two primary categories: first, active officers with the limited qualifications set forth, or second, civilians with similar qualifications but with no practical knowledge of actual police work.

The approach toward self-defense training in police work has, in the main, maintained theoretical methods. Example: Popular judo-type throws are extremely difficult for one who has not undergone constant training, as they involve split-second timing and sharp reflexes. Obviously, the average law enforcement officer does not have this ability.

During the early part of November 1978, a classic example of insufficient knowledge in self-defense methods for law enforcement was depicted on one of the major American television networks. A trespasser had just leapt over the high fence surrounding the White House. He was dressed in a karate-type uniform. The man was immediately ringed by the White House detail and there appeared to be at least ten or 12 men involved in the apprehension. The subject, quite possibly a mental case, commenced to defend himself by using various karate-type kicks and strikes. Some of the officers attempted to poke and strike at the man with short staffs in a highly amateurish manner. It was only after the subject slipped and fell after a faulty kick that the men were able to pounce upon him—their sheer numbers, of course, finally subdued the offender. The TV report, also seen in Tokyo, showed two or three men who had been injured in the fray being led away. The sad fact was that the arrested man had on only a white belt. Although it was apparent that the man knew *some* elementary form of karate, he was by no means an expert. He could have been apprehended or subdued very simply if the officers were sufficiently trained in the use of, say, the bo. The foregoing scene graphically illustrates that even top U.S. enforcement agencies lack proper training in self-defense, and it can be concluded that training in the U.S. is outmoded in many instances.

Japan

The Japanese police officer may elect to take a number of courses in self-defense training after being assigned to regular duties, since they are required to maintain proficiency in their chosen art through regular training until well into their 40s. Generally, an officer will pursue one of the major arts such as judo, kendo, and aikido, at the Tokyo Metropolitan Police Department. (Karate is not one of the approved arts under the official curriculum.) The instructors, for the most part, are senior officers who possess higher black belt rankings. Training halls are considered a normal facility in all police stations. Officers train either before or after duty hours.

Police schools and academies, such as the Nakano Police School, are fully staffed by both police and non-police instructors possessing high degrees in their respective arts—normally, seventh and eighth dans—and are ably assisted by qualified assistants of the lower dans. Budo training is taken very seriously, along with other required police subjects.

The well-known Task Force (Riot Control) Division, comprising some 4,500 specially-selected officers within the MPD, undergo regular training in the arts. The Yoshinkan system of aikido has been the official method of the MPD for the past 20 years. A number of officers—approximately ten in a group—are carefully selected to undergo aikido training for a period of nine months to a year. Upon completion, these officers attain black belt rankings and are then reassigned to the Task Force. With the formation of the Special Police (SP) detail, a unit patterned after the U.S. Secret Service's White House detail, a major requirement was that members must possess a minimum of a third dan in aikido, judo, or kendo to be eligible for consideration. Aikido graduates of the Task Force are required to attend semiannual refresher training at the Nakano Police School.

Budo training in Japanese police work combines judo and kendo, resulting in the subject of *jukendo*, a combination of the two. These two arts were the forerunners of police defensive tactics—arts which were popular during the early days of judo evolvement. Around 1947, instructors attempted to create a new system using some 32 basic forms or patterns; it was called *taihojutsu*—meaning roughly, "arresting techniques." These two systems still exist to date with slight improvements. The major weaknesses noted in the two arts: they were created mainly by judo and kendo instructors, so theoretical techniques evolved into set patterns and no provisions were made to defend from all directions, as would be the case under a practical situation. In other words, the student was taught only forms or patterns.

The training, while far superior to ones in the U.S. and elsewhere, is still considered undesirable. Pure judo, kendo, aikido, etc., cannot and should not be considered as being perfectly suited as defensive tactics for law enforcement personnel. An uncontrolled kick as utilized in karate can maim or even kill an opponent; by the same token, an aikido-type lock can very easily dislocate or break bones if not controlled properly. And, of course, not knowing how to fall correctly can also result in injuries of a serious nature.

The heavy emphasis of a senior instructor's speciality cannot be easily changed by others—more so if he is the head instructor for training. Since knowledge in several arts would be required, no one has been able to completely devise a change over the years, and a stagnant situation exists. What has evolved, at best, are strong sporting judoists and kendoists among police officers intent only on winning events. This is a far cry from its major purpose, that of self-defensive tactics for *all* officers.

The Keijutsu Concept

Keijutsu include techniques distilled from the author's personal knowledge and studies of several arts. The ultimate objective is to train the individual to use just enough force to effectively subdue or restrain a subject without seriously injuring same, and protecting himself from possible harm while doing so. Keijutsu attempts to offset many of the deficiencies found in defensive training tactics today. It incorporates the open-end principle to enable updating of certain techniques without destroying the basic concept. A discussion of techniques concerning Keijutsu will not be elaborated upon at this time since the book is directed at the general readership. Keijutsu is, and will be restricted to only those directly concerned with official law enforcement duties, as the author feels that they should be trained in a superior manner, much more than a student undergoing outside training in the arts. Officers should be considered specialists.

GLOSSARY

Ai: Matching, even; where two individuals face each other using the same stance (e.g., right vs. right). The opposite is *gyaku.*

Atemi: A strike.

*Chudan uke: A block protecting the midsection of the body; can also mean a blow to the midsection as in *chudan tsuki.*

*Gedan uke: A low block; can also refer to low kicks as in *gedan keri (geri).*

Gyaku: Opposite, reverse; where two individuals face each other using different stances (e.g., left vs. right). The opposite is *ai.*

Hanmi: A three-quarter stance in which the upper body faces straight while the feet (one in front, one to the side) form a rough right angle; also referred to as the half-body stance.

Hidari: Left.

Hiji: Elbow.

Ikkajyo: First classification; one of the basic aikido forms.

*Jodan uke: Overhead block; can also refer to blows to the face and head as in *jodan tsuki.*

Jushin: Balance, the center of gravity.

Kamae: Stance; thus, a *hidari hanmi kamae* is a left three-quarter stance. Also used as a command.

*Kansetsu: Joints, as in the arms or the legs.

Kata te: A single hand.

Kime waza: Final locking technique.

Kiritsu: To stand at attention, heels together and toes forming a 45-degree angle. A command.

Kokyu: As used in aikido, a state of compatibility with the movements of another; "fitting in;" to go with the grain. The Keijutsukai are strong advocates of this principle, used in practical application.

*Kosetsu: Fracture.

Koshi: The hips and/or lower back.

*Kote: Wrist; also called *tekubi.*

Kote gaeshi: Outer wristlock throw.

Ma-ai: In aikido, the proper operating distance between two partners for successful execution of any technique.

Marui:	Circular, round; a principle in aikido techniques.
Migi:	Right.
Mochi:	To grasp or hold with the hand(s).
Nage:	A throw.
Nikajyo:	Second classification; one of the basic aikido forms.
Omote:	Front.
Ryote:	Both hands.
Sankajyo:	Third classification; one of the basic aikido forms.
Seiza:	Kneeling position; also used as a command to kneel.
Shiho nage:	A directional throw, so named because it can be executed in any direction (see chart on pages 22 and 23).
Shikko:	Walking on the knees, an exercise.
Shime:	A lock; thus, a *kansetsu shime waza* is a joint lock.
Shite:	The defender, also called *tori*. The one who executes an aikido technique in practice.
Shomen:	Front, also called *omote*.
Te:	Hand; *ryote* is both hands.
Tegatana:	Hand blade; striking with the outer edge of the open palm.
Tekubi:	Wrist; also called *kote*.
Tsuki:	A thrust, as with the fingers.
Uchi:	A strike; usually refers to a strike with the hand blade *(tegatana)*.
Uke:	The attacker or receiver of an aikido technique in practice.
Ukemi:	Falling techniques, used when thrown in practice.
Ura:	Back; *omote* is front.
Uraken:	Back fist.
Waza:	Any technique form.
Yoi:	Prepare; a command.
Yokomen:	The side of the face or temple region.
Yonkajyo:	Fourth classification; a basic aikido form.

*These terms are not used in this book. Knowing them, however, may prove useful in further aikido studies.